10 TIPS FOR LEADING IN THE MIDDLE EAST

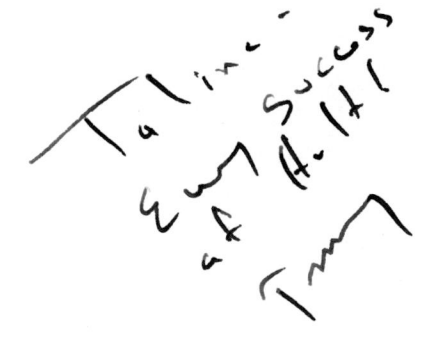

DR. TOMMY WEIR

Copyright © 2013 Dr. Tommy Weir
All rights reserved.

ISBN: 1482396815
ISBN 13: 9781482396812

Library of Congress Control Number: 2013910237
Createspace Independent Publishing Platform
North Charleston, South Carolina

DEDICATION

As strange as it may sound, I am dedicating this book to the people of Lebanon. You opened my eyes to a bigger world and showed me a path to the whole of the Middle East, which taught me a new way to lead. Without you, this book would not exist; you started it all and made me into an American Arab (an American living in the Arab world by choice). Because of this beginning with you I strongly feel I am part of the community that is the Arab world.

ACKNOWLEDGMENTS

I'd like to thank Wassim for his constant pushing to see this book move from an idea into reality.

To the thousands of you who contributed through your stories, experiences, and insights over this past decade, thank you. These tips would not exist without you.

Shukran Hyati, the love of my life, thank you for being my cheerleader and putting up with my years of research and writing when you would have preferred to have my time with you and our kids.

And finally, thanks are due to the Polo Club, where I penned most of this conversation while sitting by the pool.

TABLE OF CONTENTS

TIP #1: AVOID LEADERSHIP COLONIALISM — 1

TIP #2: DISCOVER WHAT IT MEANS TO LEAD IN A FIRST-GENERATION CORPORATE SOCIETY — 21

TIP #3: SPEED UP WHEN DEALING WITH THE YOUTH BULGE — 37

TIP #4: RECEIVE THE SOUL WHILE PERCEIVING THE APPEARANCE — 53

TIP #5: REMEMBER THAT THE FUTURE IS NOT MEASURED BY THE QUARTER — 63

TIP #6: ASK, "FATHER, MAY I?" — 77

TIP #7: THANK GOD IT'S FRIDAY — 89

TIP #8: REALIZE THAT DIVERSITY IS MULTIDIMENSIONAL — 103

TIP #9: BE CAREFUL—THERE IS NO "GET OUT OF JAIL FREE" CARD — 111

TIP #10: HAVE A CUP OF COFFEE — 121

INTRODUCTION

Valentine's Day 1999, while staying in the mountains of Lebanon, my understanding of leadership and life changed. As strangers were feeding me what then seemed to be bizarre food, it dawned on me that leading is different here.

You may be asking, "How do you make the jump from food to leadership being different?" Let me tell you a story to bring this to life.

At that time I was finishing my doctoral studies in strategic leadership and had already become a "leadership junkie"—you might even say "leadership nerd"; everywhere I went and in whatever I did, I analyzed and dissected how people led. This hobby continues with me to this day.

Arriving in Lebanon late at night and experiencing what seemed like a party (I subsequently learned that this is just a simple Lebanese dinner that stretches until the wee hours of the morning), the next day I found myself at my first *meze*. As my hosts were teaching me about their culture and food, I was also learning something entirely different. I was learning that leading is not the same all over the world.

The culture, the habits, and the society are very different in the Middle East, and that means that the way to lead should be different as well. At that time I was thinking about a doctoral seminar I had just completed in which we had discussed contingency theory—the idea that the optimal way to lead is dependent on the environment. If this was true from one organization to another, how much more would it hold true from one *country* to another? I could not wait to share these thoughts with the chair of my doctoral committee.

By the time I got back to the United States and could see him, I had fallen in love with Lebanon; a few years later I fell in love *in* Lebanon and grew deeply to love the whole region. I changed the focus of my studies to leading in the Arab world. And this altered the course of my life.

As soon as I could relocate to the region full-time, I did.

I set out to understand how to lead in the Middle East. This passion and focus has allowed me to interview business leaders from every country in the region; to move through the region, making a home on both sides – the Levant and GCC; and to spend numerous days and nights—adding up to months—in most of the countries. This added up to more than a decade of research and advising leading local, regional, and multinational businesses.

Given this focus, I am regularly asked, "From your experience and research, what does it take to be a good leader in the Middle East?" So, think of this book as a conversation over coffee in which we discuss that very topic and in which I share the experiences and insights I've gathered over the last decade while researching, practicing, and experiencing leadership in the Middle East.

So, whether you are an expat, who is the primary audience, from the region, or merely curious about this topic and a seeker of leadership knowledge, you will find what you are looking for – tips on how to lead in the Middle East.

One last point before we pour our coffee. I would be remiss if I did not address those who might quickly say, "There is no

INTRODUCTION

such thing as one Middle East." They are correct. Each and every country is distinct, and in my research I've discovered that each has a unique approach to leadership.

This same argument holds true for my home country of the United States, and probably any other region around the world; for instance, it is definitely true in Europe as well. People from one country argue they are different from others, and they are. None of us lives in exactly the same culture. Culture varies from city to city, from family to family, and sometimes even from individual to individual.

Being fully aware of differences among the Gulf Cooperation Council (GCC), the Levant, and Egypt, and even within the GCC among Saudis, Emiratis, Kuwaitis, Omanis, Bahrainis, and Qataris, in my years of research I've discovered principal similarities when it comes to leading. Rather than addressing this from a theoretical level, let's be practical and see the areas of commonality. Together they are enough to plead for this book.

At a metalevel, this book is addressing what was once called Western Asia or the Near East (excluding Turkey). We now identify it through its subdivided areas: the Levant, Egypt, northern Africa, and the GCC. So when I use the terms *Middle East*, *Arab World*, and *Arabia*, I am generically addressing a broad geographic area. Only when I refer to the GCC am I being specific to one part of the region.

Grab your coffee and let's have a conversation about what it takes to be a great leader in the Middle East.

TIP #1:

AVOID LEADERSHIP COLONIALISM

There is a danger in trying to import leadership approaches in the same way the Gulf Cooperation Council (GCC) exports oil. The practice of oil exportation is chock-full of consistencies, no matter where the final destination is or what the end usage of that oil may be. But leadership is a different commodity, and leaders shouldn't expect to be able to import non-native and historical leadership practices—or Western-orientated models of leadership—to a distinct work environment thousands of miles away.

When Bob Willett stepped off the plane to take the helm as CEO of the Al-Futtaim Group, a conglomerate of over forty companies across various industry sectors, he brought with him his tried-and-true "playbook." He came to the region with an accomplished executive pedigree, having most recently been CEO of Best Buy, a fifty-billion-dollar consumer electronics corporation with 167,000 employees. I am sure he thought, "Why should it be any different here in the Middle

East? I will do what has always brought me success." So, he embarked upon his plan, which included several "housekeeping" strategies. Expected to lead the group into a new era of positive change, his importing of non-native leadership practices earned him an unexpected early return ticket home, not even completing one year as CEO.

If, therefore, you are tempted to import foreign models designed and taught at the best Western business schools, beware of the practical risks. On a time scale, these risks will take you from only the possibility of an error in judgment to probable failure.

As either an Arab national or an expatriate, if you see outside leadership success as opening the floodgates for similar success in this region, you will cause complete frustration for those being led. All that this train of thought does is identify a model that has succeeded in some other location for another organization. The Middle East workforce simply is not composed of "more people, somewhere else"; it differs fundamentally from that of the developed economies with respect to culture, organizational mind-set, work attitudes, and familial approaches. The first tip for successfully leading in the Middle East is to adapt your leadership approach for the region.

To date, most of the modern management models and practices are based on Western concepts. But whatever the origin of these concepts, you should be critical of the tendency to import non-native models and practices with little or no thought to their adaptability to local environments. Leadership is essentially what is practiced in reality; it is not a theoretical construct. Continuing to import leadership practices in the same way that the GCC exports oil has not proved to be a winning strategy—certainly not in the long term.

My aim is to help expatriate and local leaders alike overcome their dependence on easy but unsustainable solutions inspired by leadership models imported from elsewhere. The net effect of that approach has been to sideline local leadership structures that I consider key to establishing leadership practices adapted to changing local conditions.

WHEN THE CONTEXT CHANGES

Pick a city in the region, any city—Dubai, Abu Dhabi, Doha, Riyadh, Cairo, Beirut. What similarities, if any, do you see between that city and, say, Ohio (a state in the middle of the United States)? Do you think the business environment in Dubai, any city within the GCC, or any Middle Eastern city differs radically from that of Ohio? The obvious answer is a resounding yes. The business environment in the Middle East as a whole is vastly different from that of Ohio today and even more so from what it was like sixty years ago.

Yet we rely on leadership thinking that comes straight out of the 1940s and '50s—and the middle of the United States, from Ohio. The world then was still reeling from the effects of the Second World War, and much of the thinking about leadership and management that came out of that era was shaped by a military mind-set working in a mechanistic environment. The Ohio State Leadership Studies focused on how leaders could satisfy common group needs. The findings indicated that the two most important dimensions in leadership included: "initiating structure" and "consideration".

How can such a model work in the Middle East, especially since several countries in the region had not yet gained their independence by the close of World War II? The majority of the Middle East was not even involved in World War II.

The truth is that after the war the United States played a pivotal role in revitalizing the world economy; it also helped reform modern industrial practices, ideas, and approaches—including thinking about leadership. Since the early work in modern leadership research was US-centric, Western ideals remain embedded in the core of leadership thinking and practices. Fast-forward to modern-day Arabia and the same, largely Western-driven leadership models are still being propagated, even by non-American firms. This approach falls short in terms of leading where the field of play has changed while much of the thinking about leadership has not.

Don't get me wrong, the famed Ohio State University studies and others like them are well-grounded. They served well the relatively homogenous ex-military workforce of Ohio. But company executives face far greater diversity in the Middle East than in 1950s Ohio. This is true with respect to nationality, cultural background, and, of course, religion. In contrast, how many Muslims do you think lived and worked in Ohio in 1948? Clearly, the Ohio studies were not designed for the modern Middle Eastern corporate context, which is young, fast-paced, ambiguous, complex, and comprising multiple nationalities (in the GCC). The danger is in misguided leaders imposing foreign leadership models and, in so doing, imperiling the health of their businesses.

The Ohio studies supplied valid constructs that explained patterns of management behavior in a thoroughly mechanistic way. Management techniques have come a long way since then, even in the United States. Researchers have been able to build on their predecessors' work and to accumulate new knowledge of their own. One good example is the Michigan State University leadership studies, which built on the findings and analyses of the Ohio State studies, which were followed by Douglas McGregor's Theory X, Theory Y, and so forth. Even in today's leadership studies the foundation of the Ohio State studies remains intact. Despite these and other advances, both the thinking behind the research and the practice of leadership have created the foundation for Western leadership thinking and practice that include an Anglo-Saxon model of traits, a militaristic influence, industrialization, and a homogenous environment.

When the context changes, shouldn't our leadership approach change along with it?

THE ORIGIN OF LEADERSHIP COLONIALISM

Historically, a sizable portion of the Arabic-speaking world was, at one point or another, ruled by a Western colonial power or fell under some foreign mandate. Leaving the morality of colonial empires aside, this short-lived domination created new channels for cultural exchange and the assimilation of new (typically Western) approaches to leading. This legacy includes an importation of leadership approaches and a willingness to look outside for management practices. Unfortunately, leadership colonialism still exists, causing a decline in the local traditions of leadership, and its comprehensive impact.

These Western approaches tend to conflict with the local patterns and customs and do not lead to reaching full leadership potential. There is a dichotomy between the adoption of Western models and the desire to retain culturally aligned approaches. The Western approaches appeal to the perception of prestige, but they are not relevant and appropriate for today's Middle Eastern business advantage.

In the 2000s, a number of leading organizations invested over a million dollars apiece in so-called global leadership development programs hoping to improve leadership capability in their organizations, only to be disappointed later with the results. They then had to deal with failed investments, having put good money into a program that yielded nothing close to what they expected—namely, a new crop of world-caliber senior business leaders. Business leaders should instead build on existing patterns of leadership and local demographic realities—in other words, they should be using indigenous social levers that are already in place. Leaders have to recognize that the *what* of leadership alone can't substitute for the exciting possibilities that a grasp of the context-driven *how* can offer.

OVERCOMING LEADERSHIP COLONIALISM

This is, without a doubt, easier said than done. Organizational leaders in the Middle East need to recognize how unique the regional work culture and environment is. Then, instead of immediately relying on one of the prestigious or popular Western-based leadership approaches, they need to focus on determining what the real leadership challenges are and what type of leader is needed. Then and only then will an organization be in a position to mitigate the risks and to create a leadership approach that is relevant.

To lead successfully, it is imperative that the leader gain specific understanding of the interplay of societal and workplace variables, which do not operate in isolation from each other. Determining how these variables influence further the conduct of one's business and workforce will enable the leader to introduce more productive ideas into the current model, whatever that may be. The object is for the leader to position him- or herself to meet the complex challenges of both leadership and the region by first factoring in the cultural idiosyncrasies of the organization's workforce and, more widely, the workforce.

The leadership context in Ohio and Michigan in the 1950s was vastly different from that of the Middle East today. For that matter, today's Middle East is unique, differing from other markets around the world given its current market life cycle, abrupt development, and demographics. Yet most of the leadership and management ideas continue to be imported wholesale from somewhere else. Why?

ADAPT YOUR LEADERSHIP APPROACH

Given the clear plea to avoid leadership colonialism, business leaders in the Middle East need to adapt their leadership approach to fit the demands and needs of the region, and the local workforce realities, while focusing on the organization's strategic vision and goals. Many leaders have argued that leadership is the same all over the world, and that there is an overarching global leadership approach. This simply is not true when it comes to actually leading, as it needs to be oriented toward the specifics of those being led.

There is no escaping the fact that there is global consistency in *what* leadership is, as every company requires leaders to help direct and fulfill its strategic vision. However, the confusion comes in mistaking the *what* and the *how* of leadership, as there are vast differences in terms of styles of leadership between focus on task versus context.

Imagine yourself traveling abroad for the first time, and you decide to buy a Coca-Cola. Before this experience, your assumption was that Coke was the same all over the world. Every advertisement you've seen consistently shows Coca-Cola's trademark red color and the bottle's contents to be dark caramel, giving the impression that Coke's ingredients are the same everywhere. Now you discover something new about the famed Coke drink: the taste varies greatly from one region to another. In other words, the *what* of Coke is the same wherever you live—a soft drink to quench thirst—but *how* it tastes varies by region to match local tastes.

The same holds true on the question of leadership. Here is a simplified definition of leadership that we can think about: leadership is what a leader does and how he does it to and for his followers to achieve a common goal. In this rudimentary sense, leadership may strike you as some sort of universal concept. This is where the *how* comes in; it pertains to the concrete manifestation of your leadership. Clearly, we are no longer in the zone of generalities.

There are four components inherent in this definition of leading—the leader, the follower(s), the interaction between the two, and the goal. As they appear to be consistent, leaders attempt to import and export the practice of leading from one market to the next even though each of the components can vary dramatically from culture to culture and from one organization to the next.

This is the practical reason why current business leaders in the Middle East must modify their approaches. There is no getting around it—the "flavor" has to match local tastes and expectations. Inevitably, how the leader leads and provides direction to the followers should vary by region.

AVOID LEADERSHIP COLONIALISM

The flavor of leading should be suitably adjusted to local tastes as well. For example, a universal practice of effective leaders is to provide clarity and direction to followers—that is, the workforce. This principle—the *what* of leading—is global, but *how* the leader gives direction should vary by region.

I'll never forget the panic and confusion I felt on my first visit to the headquarters of Savola, one of the world's leading edible oil companies, based in Jeddah, Saudi Arabia. I had been to Jeddah many times prior to this trip, so I was comfortable with my surroundings, but not with the directions I received.

Talking to the vice president I was about to meet, I asked, "How do I get to your office?" Without hesitation he replied, "Oh its easy; are you taking a taxi?"

"Yes."

"Then tell the taxi to go right out of the hotel, until you come to the roundabout that has an empty field next to where the toy store used to be; we are the big building next to that."

I paused, waiting for him to laugh, hoping this was a joke. When he didn't, I asked, "What are those directions again?" and he repeated, "Go to the roundabout that has an empty field next to where the toy store used to be, we are the big building next to that field."

"The taxi driver will know this?" I asked.

"Of course, Insha'Allah," he said, as if to comfort me.

Now panicking, I left my hotel room wondering, "When was the toy store there? Last month? Last year? A decade ago?"

This vague landmark-oriented direction was very disconcerting for me. I am used to exact addresses—and maps, if possible—rather than landmarks. I was a little nervous climbing into a taxi armed only with these vague directions, but we surprisingly managed to reach our destination. Apparently, the directions were crystal clear to the taxi driver.

9

You see, leaders can't just dish out directions with little or no thought to the actual practices of those they must count on to execute their directives, those they purport to lead. Following our analogy, do your followers prefer detailed street names and numbers, or are they visually reliant on landmarks? Do they consult Google Maps to get detailed sets of directions, or simply process the journey one step at a time? Leaders simply have to understand and embrace this level of difference and translate this everyday example of going from one location to another into how they communicate expectations in the workplace. You cannot successfully lead others without adapting your leadership approach to the region.

In my experience, the very notion of adapting leadership to the context is an obvious piece of advice to an expatriate, although it is not always heeded. Yet, it is equally important for the Western-educated and Western-exposed Arab national who has potentially worked outside the region, or for a multinational corporation, to do the same. The adaptation is deeper than the background of where the leader comes from; it is systemic, and built on what we believe about leading.

With the case clearly made as to why leading in the Middle East requires adapting one's leadership approach, let's answer the obvious question: How can the leader adapt his or her approach in order to make it relevant?

HOW TO ADAPT YOUR APPROACH

The forcing of a leadership concept from one culture onto another is something that is easy to fall into. Leaders need to be very wary of the assumption that their way is the best way. This means making sure that they do more than import an idea from a distant land and apply it as the answer in the local or regional environment. Leaders need to respond to local needs and make this market, the Middle East, the focal point of leadership.

UNDERSTAND THE REALITY OF THE CONTEXT

Just as streetwise business operators get to know the customers and sophisticated organizations invest in consumer insights, good leaders make it their business to know the people they are leading. Mere speculation about their needs, characteristics, and aspirations will not be enough. Leaders have to go beyond speculation; the call is to explore, without exception, all the causal factors that might shape performance inside the organization.

Foremost in the leader's mind should be devising an effective plan of approach. The four elements that leaders have to consider are employees' unique backgrounds, their thinking patterns, native societal structures, and the dominant religion of the culture.

1. *Employees' Unique Backgrounds*

Good leaders are not afraid to tackle issues relating to their employees' backgrounds. On the contrary, they discover and scrutinize them, because they know how useful (or destabilizing) they can be. They want to know how their employees think and behave. Furthermore, leaders must be conscious of their own assumptions as they go about shaping the team they hope to successfully lead. To that end, they can safely set aside older constructs of questionable value. They do all this in order to enrich and deepen their current understanding of the way in which their organization should be led.

As strange as it is, there are still leaders around today who see little value in exploring the individual/personal dimensions of their operations. This inability or unwillingness to factor in the cultural heritage that each employee brings with him or her to work can cause confusion and miscommunication.

Many times there is great confusion in the leader-member exchange when the leader fails to take into consideration the employees' backgrounds. It is common sense to do so, and it should be a universal practice, but in the challenging Middle Eastern work environment it needs to be practiced at a greater level of intensity. Here are a series of questions to aid you in getting to know your employees:

- What demographic factors are shaping your workforce?
- What cultural factors do your employees bring into the workforce?
- What larger societal factors (backgrounds) are active in your workforce?
- How was your employees' understanding of customer orientation developed?
- How was their performance understanding developed?
- Where does the employees' understanding of an organization/corporation come from?

We are not out of the woods yet. There are two glaring risks in this area. For one thing, considering an employee's unique background is heavily reliant upon anthropology and sociology, a skill set not traditionally taught or practiced in business schools. And two, without broad regional exposure as an expatriate, including significant experience in various local relationships, it is difficult but necessary to put aside individual experiences and to be able to question why things are as they are in the Middle East culture—and to draw conclusions that inform how to lead. Why are things as they are in this particular culture? Without some insight into this question—with local assistance, no doubt—experience has shown that leading can quickly become problematic.

Remember that this practice is for the Middle Eastern leader as much as or more than the expatriate. When an expatriate enters a foreign market, there is at least a minimal awareness that employees' backgrounds will be different. When a leader is leading in his or her home country, however, the assumption is that this leader is fully aware of the employees' backgrounds, but the hierarchy and the breadth of the society and the workforce mean that what might appear to be similar on the surface may actually be different. The usual assumption is that, of all people, this national leader is the person who fully understands the significance and potential impact of employees' backgrounds. For example, if all employees grew up in the same country and speak a common language, on the surface it seems similar. But if the leader has greater international exposure through education and experience, then he or she needs to be aware of this bias when leading.

I've spent countless hours advising national leaders on how to overcome this bias, because the leader and led are often very different. Take as an example, Sherif, an Egyptian who is leading in Egypt. His claim is that because he is Egyptian (albeit Western-educated and with a decade of experience abroad) he understands the Egyptian workforce. In reality, Sherif is barely coping with the behavioral traits of his followers; such traits are clearly different from what he had learned about while studying at Durham University and working abroad for a multinational corporation. And yet, simply by pausing to understand who his workforce is, Sherif was able to correct any possible distortions in his views and adapt his leadership approach.

There are additional aspects to consider when examining a particular region or society:

- What societal (and parental) support exists for corporate life, and why is this support as it is?
- What general beliefs and "stories" are shaping the workers' attitudes?
- What, historically, has been the educational model and approach?
- What experience has the individual had?
- What is the perceived value of workplace performance in the local culture?
- What work patterns have existed in the region in recent history?
- Where does the culture of the society's current business life cycle lie?

A starting point for understanding your employees is to go back and read the résumés of your "inherited" employees—that is, those who were hired before you took over as leader. Take time to get to know who you are leading.

A few years back, I was having coffee with the CEO of a global telecom company that has a presence in the GCC, and he described what seemed to him to be unique but is in fact commonplace. Recognizing that the company would be having an extremely diverse workforce, he asked the strategic question, "What does it mean to have multiple nationalities and employees with varied backgrounds working together?" He explained that the company's employees came from numerous backgrounds but were now all working together within the GCC. In fact, the company boasted of having thirty-five different nationalities in the workforce, and all but one was working outside of its home country. The CEO recognized this reality and hit the pause button to explore what this meant for how each of the company's leaders should lead. He explored the fundamental questions mentioned earlier, and concluded that the company needed to adapt their global leadership approach to be relevant locally.

An effective leader will explore all the important questions as I have delineated them in this chapter, constantly digging deeper into cultural backgrounds. The leader's goal is to adapt as far as possible the company's leadership approach according to his or her findings in order to drive greater performance.

2. *Employee's Thinking Patterns*

Human cognition is different everywhere in the world. Social psychologists have discovered that at the most elementary level, so-called Asians (including most of Arabia) and Westerners maintain different systems of thought. For example, Westerners have a strong interest in categorization, which helps them to know what rules to apply to the objects in question. And they rely on logic to play a role in problem solving.

Conversely, Asians attend to objects in their broad context and how they relate to one another. The need to explore locality in relationship to leadership is apparent through this description of the Western and Asian basic thought processes. Leaders would be wise to consider the system of thought as they explore their employees' background.

3. *Employee's Native Societal Structures*

Social structures are also distinct among various cultures and environments. They affect how a leader leads and what the follower needs from the leader. The way in which groups relate to each other is based on relatively enduring patterns of behavior and relationships through family and schooling within the social system. The social norms embed in social systems in such a way that they shape the behavior of leaders and employees within them. In and of themselves, social structures are very complex. This complexity intensifies when attempting to cross cultures or integrate various social norms and patterns. We carry our cultural values everywhere we go. The trick is learning how to understand and appreciate others native social structures.

4. *The Dominant Religion of the Nurturing Culture*

As a factor in leadership, religion entails far more than rituals and spirituality. Unlike the Western idea of the world being divided into two comprehensive domains—one sacred and the other profane—in the Middle East religion presents a common quality for societal character. Religion is a communal system of belief based on moral codes, practices, values, institutions, traditions, and rituals. It shapes personal attitudes and prescribes group rituals—in short, it is a way of life, indeed more so in the Middle East than in, say, northern Europe.

Unlike the homogenous impact of religion when operating across European and American markets, in the Middle East Islam impacts personal attitudes and practices, and to a great extent work behavior. A good business leader understands the broader impact of religion on people as members of society.

In effect, you are creating a workplace dossier, which is a collection of detailed information about your employees, together with a synopsis of the collected insights. This is more than a résumé; a workplace dossier contains information from multiple sources. Much of these insights will come via conversations with your employees through which you seek to understand their background. This dossier will serve you well as a leader in being able to adapt your leadership approach and ultimately motivate your team to top performance.

MAINTAIN FOCUS ON CULTURAL HERITAGE AND AN ORGANIZATIONAL FUTURE

In addition to understanding the uniqueness of employees' experience and developmental environment, the leader has the obligation to create a bridge between the culture of the employees and the organization so that he or she can graft the employees' local identity onto the corporate environment. Success resides in knowing both sides and how to connect one with the other. One of the more important elements in such grafting is to understand the depth and development of the societal background. This will facilitate bridge building and help leverage the most effective leadership approach. Most global leadership approaches routinely hold the unconscious assumptions that employees:

- were educated, most likely through public education, in a modern classroom that utilized active learning (as opposed to rote memorization),
- have an understanding of the idea of organizational life as it is constructed via extracurricular activities at an elementary level and supported in most social interactions,
- have a consistent underpinning stemming from the influence of a Judeo-Christian ethic absorbed through educational programs and cultural rhythms,
- will pursue and be supported in their development as leaders,
- have an understanding of operations from their first jobs held, and

- operate from tightly aligned commonalities with co-workers in their organization.

These unconscious assumptions do not align with the cultural heritage of the majority of the Middle East.

An individual's hypothesis about his or her environment is not only a basis for describing the environment but also seriously influences the way the individual behaves toward the environment. The uniqueness of individual experiences creates the uniqueness of personality. Success in leading comes as organizations are able to graft the organizational environment and employees' cultural backgrounds together. Attention needs to be given to focus on the organization's future and the cultural heritage of the employees while bringing the two together.

MODIFY THE LEADERSHIP APPROACH AS NEEDED

When we look at leadership, pretty much everything that we've been taught or propagated comes largely from North America, supplemented by western Europe. We can spend all day generating proof cases in an attempt to support preexisting assumptions about leading. But when we push that away for a second and look at sociological data, it prompts us to say, wait a minute—leaders need to modify their approach.

The next step after compiling a workplace dossier is to discover how your existing leadership approach can be modified to maximize its impact. Here, leaders are supposed to assess regional realities and investigate the factors for better localization and a more effective leadership model.

This may require that you use your imagination in order to move away from the "import" model and to adapt your leadership approach for the reality of the workforce. Your leadership

AVOID LEADERSHIP COLONIALISM

solutions and methods need to be created for the market. Leaders need to look beyond their current hypotheses about leading and explore the causal factors in the workforce and workplace with the purpose of constructing an appropriate solution.

This first tip for leading in the Middle East requires that you start by identifying the rhythms and nuances that are present in the local workforce and culture. Next, focus on understanding the leadership needs, and establish where they originated from and why they are as they are. Only then should you put energy into seeking the solution of how to lead—adapting your leadership approach. This is especially true when people are mistakenly importing Western approaches to leading without giving consideration to local cultural rhythms.

TIP #2:

DISCOVER WHAT IT MEANS TO LEAD IN A FIRST-GENERATION CORPORATE SOCIETY

Over the years, I have watched both national and expatriate business leaders assume their posts across the Middle East. As we saw in the previous tip, too often they neglect to appreciate the character of the workforce. For example, this means having to rely principally on the first generation of employees to penetrate the private sector—that is, corporate life. Unfortunately, most attempt to lead without understanding the reality of leading in a first-generation corporate society.

The world seems to have a split between existing corporate societies, where the private sector has been a dominant part of life for multiple generations, and first-generation corporate societies in other parts of the world. The primary difference between existing corporate societies and first-generation corporate societies is that the former emerged during the era of industrialization while the latter have remained agricultural, government-employment, and cottage-industry societies until very recently, at which time they began to experience massive development, bypassing the Industrial Revolution route.

While the Middle East boasts a few mature family businesses, some of which go back generations, most in the current workforce are among the first members from their family to work in a corporate environment. They have historically worked in the public sector or small *dukkan*-style businesses (those similar to cottage industries). Only recently have they started to populate the corporate sector. The consequence has been that only now are social and family support/development systems being built for a corporate environment. On the other hand, Western societies have been involved in the corporate culture since the early 1900s, when they experienced the same migration out of agricultural, government-employment, and cottage industry societies that the Middle East is experiencing now.

THE RISE OF THE CORPORATE WORLD

It is practically impossible to account for the region's past decade of accelerated change without putting things in proper historical perspective. Since the early 1900s, Western societies have experienced unprecedented growth and moved steadily away from agriculture, government employment, and the cottage industry. It was back in 1952 when Ray Kroc began applying the thinking behind the Industrial Revolution to the process of business development and created the franchise engine, thus bringing the McDonald's fast-food chain and franchising to the world. Yet in the 1950s, many of the countries in the Middle East were still under foreign sovereignty, serving as little more than outposts and colonies for the conquering empires.

It could be argued that a "corporate" era has come into its own with the arrival of McDonald's, the symbol of structured operations meeting with everyday life. McDonald's perfected and expanded the idea of the assembly line for food production, delivery, and the franchise. If the fast-food chain ushered in the corporate era, this means the Middle East began corporatizing as recently as 1993. Accelerated growth has happened in the past decade, well after the expanse of the Industrial Revolution and the modern era.

In the Middle East, the route to the corporate society is coming via service and knowledge economies, unlike in the West, which made its transition from an agrarian society into the private sector through industry. Here the Middle East is leaping over their counterpart's journey to corporatizing and creating the appearance of similarity, yet decades of corporate practices have not been built into the rhythms and psyche of Middle Eastern society. For example, in industrialized nations, business structures stem from a mechanistic mentality, while in the Middle East business structures stem from family orientation.

This is precisely why corporate leaders working in the Middle East should familiarize themselves at least with the region's recent history of rapid growth. The important thing is that leaders open their eyes to the specific demands and expectations of employees, most of whom are from a first-generation corporate society.

THE BUSINESS MARKET LIFE CYCLE

This transition in the phase of the business market life cycle is not a new concept. We can look to history to see how other regions made this transition from a rural culture to a corporate society. The United States experienced creation of the corporate society beginning in the early twentieth century during the era of America's original industrial families—the Rockefellers, Fords, Guggenheims, Vanderbilts, Flaglers, and others. Exploring that period for insights on leading in the Middle East is far more valuable than looking at General Electric's current business model or that of other modern publicly traded entities.

In the early 1900s, 90 percent of America's workforce comprised the self-employed or farmers, and today 90 percent comprises employees working in a "corporatized" organization. So while the corporate society reality is new to the Middle East, the rise of the corporate society from the original family business and government-sector models in other regions can provide clues toward what businesses should be doing.

THE FIRST-GENERATION CORPORATE SOCIETY

Leaders need to take serious account of the mix of employees—those who are "corporate citizens" in the generational sense that I have been talking about, and those who are only first-generation corporate citizens. This is vital information for anyone who wants to lead an organization. But what should leaders be aware of when leading employees who are first-generation corporate citizens? Here are three key consequences of being a first-generation corporate society.

CORPORATE SUPPORT

The Middle East has experienced a steep climb in literacy rates over the past generation. That said, many private-sector employees grew up in homes where the parents were, at best, functionally literate. Those parents have not worked in corporate environments, and thus have had little exposure to how things work—the routines and expectations of the corporatized business setting. They are simply not familiar with standard business procedures, let alone those of a multinational corporation. This lack of exposure usually translates into an inability to advise their children on workplace habits, actions, and behaviors. As a result, employees have to rely instead on whatever workplace education they receive—or may not receive, in many cases.

CORPORATE LANGUAGE

Corporate life has its own lingo, which, ideally, is learned growing up in a corporate society before entering the workforce. Often this lingo is expressed in acronyms that can be vague, and possibly confusing, for first-generation corporate citizens. Take KPIs (key performance indicators) and PD (performance development); these are assumed to be a part of an employee's working lexicon when he or she enters the workplace. Meanings, though, have a way of extending their reach beyond traditional textbook definitions. This is because they have their roots in societal behavior inside corporate society, not just in the corporate list of abbreviations. This hardly makes them native, and they are decidedly not. And such terminology can mean more frustration than would otherwise be the case if business were simply conducted in a second language. Despite this, leaders believe that every employee should master the language of business.

When it comes to learning corporate lingo, it reminds me of the dreaded spelling test in elementary school. Often during the test I would know how to spell the word but have no idea how to use it. Corporate language is the same for first-generation corporate citizens: the importance becomes clear, but the meaning and usage remain vague.

CORPORATE RHYTHMS

Corporate life involves rhythms, routines, and expectations. It is highly structured and organized according to formal rules and procedures, with a focus on shareholders' interests. On the other hand, informal social networks and personal connections, allowing for more individuality, have historically characterized agrarian and family businesses.

When coming from a corporate society, the language and rhythms of business are built through the "growing up" years, often around the family table. Being a product of a corporatized upbringing, I was shaped by "adult" conversations about management, unions, and life working inside a corporation. It was not that different from a young boy in the Middle East sitting in the *majlis* gathering among men of common interest—other than the content of the conversation, of course.

My grandfather worked for Pillsbury, famous for its Doughboy mascot and baked goods. Since my grandfather was one of the "workers"—meaning, not a "suit"—I grew up hearing from him how bad "management" was. But my father was one of the "suits," so from him I learned the other side of corporate life. Thus, from an early age I was being shaped, without even realizing it, in the ways of the structured, corporate organization.

If I did not have that experience, I would have been left wondering about these ways or discovering them firsthand in the corporation's hallways. I would have been on my own when it came to figuring out corporate basics, operations, and how organizations work.

First-generation corporate employees, especially among burgeoning middle classes, see the world differently and behave differently from their counterparts in developed economies. In the heart of the Middle East, business leaders need to be aware of this because when an employee is hired he or she most likely has a different background from that of the manager. There is probably a difference in where each was educated, exposure to local culture, and exposure to the rest of the world. As a result, the manager may be experiencing a disconnect between his or her own corporate upbringing and what is experienced by a first-generation corporate citizen.

PERFORMANCE ORIENTATIONS

During the annual performance review process, perhaps you have had one of your employees say, "But I did everything that you asked!" As the leader, this leaves you wondering, because what you observed was mediocre at best. From your point of view, what was just described is the bare minimum to receive a rating of 3 (average) and definitely not worthy of the 5 that the employee marked on his or her self-assessment—a high score showing excellent performance.

Many leaders go ahead and give the generous 3, even if the work was not completely on the mark, because the employee did work hard—actually, *very* hard—and they want to acknowledge that hard work. This is when the real problem crops up, because in the performance review, the leader's assessment is that the work is definitely not deserving of the 5 that the employee believes he or she is entitled to. Emotions can easily flare up as the confusion sets in, leaving the leader wondering, "How in the world can you justify this?"

Part of the confusion may be related to attitudes toward performance in general. In the Middle East, as elsewhere among emerging economies, performance means different things to different people. In practice, four different performance orientations have been identified: competition, mastery, completion, and ascription. These are working concepts that you need to elaborate within your own context. Let's consider them one by one.

COMPETITION

When you hear a leader or a business make reference to being number one, being the best, or claiming some other world title, clearly the performance orientation is a competitive one. This orientation takes root where people have been directly exposed to competition. At a young age, for instance, they may have observed or participated in competitive sports and athletics. This can lead to an obsession of sorts: to these people, performance largely means beating or eliminating the competition. I perform to beat you—whoever the competition is perceived to be—inside or outside the organization. It's all about being number one, king of the hill at last! It's all about winning and others losing.

MASTERY

Closely related to competition, but with some telling differences, is mastery—otherwise known as the "quality" orientation. Here the focus is on being the best that one can be. In other words the comparison, if any, is between the individual's actual performance and future potential. There is a constant strive to improve and reach the fullest quality. "Let's get better" is the constant rallying call.

A parent might say to a son, for example, "Nasser, do better in school. If you do better, you will get to a better university. If you get to a better university, then you will find a better career." Put aside the factor of peer competition, as this game is not about beating someone else but about improving one's own personal qualities. Typically, leaders adopt this mastery orientation because their parents insisted earlier in life that they excel in school, thus instilling an internal predisposition toward "getting better."

COMPLETION

Completion is wholly different from the previous two performance orientations. Completion is doing exactly what is being asked—nothing more and nothing less. It more specifically has to do with finishing a task rather than being concerned about quality or beating the competition.

This orientation finds its origin in agricultural, rural, and cottage-industry backgrounds, where performance is often managed in time. In a rural agricultural environment, if a worker is told to go pick rice for eight hours a day, he or she will go and work for eight hours in the field. After that time has passed the task has been completed. Little or no consideration is given to the quality of the work. The worker is definitely not thinking of beating a fellow worker who may be a few rows away. The focus is simply to complete the given task.

Similarly, in a cottage-industry family business where only one person who works in the business, or perhaps works with one or two other family members, the idea is to do what's needed to earn for the day. Take, for example the owner-operator of the *dukkan* (a small neighborhood shop): the focus is on selling what is needed for the day—about completing the task. Rare is the *dukkan* owner who has competition foremost in his or her mind or is in any way obsessed with being number one.

When a person with a completion performance background joins the private-sector workforce and the leader tells him or her to perform a task, he or she will do it and then announce to the leader that it is finished, thinking all the while that this is a maximum level of performance. But if the leader comes from either a competition or mastery background, he or she will be expecting more than just the hours worked or effort put in.

The ensuing conversation might go as follows.

"But the quality isn't any good. Or, how are we going to beat our competitors?"

"But I finished it," the confused employee answers. I did what you asked." And the employee is correct in this, judging by his or her accepted measure of performance. But being *correct* about something is not the same as being *right*.

Now we are at the crux of the performance conundrum from the beginning of this section. In that example, the leader had a competition or mastery performance orientation and rated the employee's performance accordingly, with a 3. On the other hand, the employee with a completion orientation sees merely completing the task as excelling at performance and thus worthy of a score of 5.

ASCRIPTION

The fourth performance orientation, ascription, referring to what can be attributed to a person, refers to aspects of the individual background that have to do with personal or family status, importance, reputation, and the like. Ascription comes from what is recognizable by others, bringing a focus on title, business card, office location, and other outward symbols. Ascription can be summarized as those things we might tend to brag about over coffee, or more so what your father would brag about with his friends. All this is wrapped up in what others may be saying about you that affect your social status. It is easy to understand from this that ascription affects honor and shame, which it injects into overall performance.

This orientation shapes some of the ways we do business. For example, if you come from an environment that does not value titles, while in an ascription environment they matter very much, you will have to make sense of a view that is different from yours rather than forcing your performance orientation on others to drive performance.

Understanding the four performance orientations begins to explain the widespread frustration over performance rating variance. The performance conflict in the workforce is typically between a leader who either has a competition or mastery orientation and employees adhering to a completion or ascription orientation. With this understanding in mind, you are positioned to be able to mature your employees' performance orientation, which should result in performance improvement.

NURTURING PRIVATE-SECTOR ACHIEVEMENT

It goes without saying that business leaders, above all, have to cultivate followers' achievement of results. It is common in the Middle East to find technical experts occupying positions of leadership. But specialists are normally focused upon the technical aspects of the business specifically related to their area of specialty. This presents a risk, since leaders need to focus on the achievement of others. Leadership cannot forgo the responsibility of unifying the followers around the same goal and motivating them to exceed their initial expectations. In a first-generation corporate society, building other people's capability, behavior, and confidence becomes a critical factor, especially in an environment where career advancement and opportunities can be based upon nepotism and connections. Today's leaders have no choice but to develop achievement-oriented, results-oriented, and driven workers.

The good leader in the Middle East acts as a bridge builder to a corporate orientation so that employees can succeed in this realm. To lead in a first-generation corporate society, you will need to unfreeze employees' attitudes and values; this, in turn, allows the parties involved to confirm the mission at hand and to possibly modify previously held norms that have proven less effective. This type of leader can change the employees mind-set because, if anything, employees may be starting to see things in a new light. In other words, the leader intellectually stimulates employees and changes their mind-set by encouraging them to see things in a new light and to question old assumptions.

If you are leading employees who are from a first-generation corporate society, then reorient your leadership style to act as a coach or mentor. Your task now is to help your employees embrace the language and rhythms of corporate life until such ideas become second nature to them. Successful leaders are not only fully aware of the issues related to first-generation corporate society but must also invest their time in developing the orientations that will best serve the corporation. This may entail having to explain the routines, jargon, and actions of business, but—more important—why they exist and the benefits of each. In other words, the leader should act also as a type of mentor in order to get maximum performance from the company's workforce.

One night, watching the legendary Coach K, Mike Krzyzewski, rule the sidelines at the Duke University versus United Arab Emirates basketball game in Dubai, left me inspired about great coaching. That night I thought, "If businesses had championship coaches, what would be the result?"

Typically, organizational coaching approaches do not use athletic coaching models to get their points across. They see the role more as listening than as problem solving. Most corporate coaching solutions are designed to enable the "coachee" to look at the present situation from various angles for better recognition of the problems and for potential solutions that may not have been thought of previously. This is a quite different from what Coach K was doing on the sidelines at that game in Dubai.

One of the all-time best basketball coaches, John Wooden of UCLA, has said that a coach is a teacher. Marshall Goldsmith, who advises top corporate executives, insists that the coach's core mission is to offer executive advice. This is the athletic coaching approach: acting as a teacher. And such an approach is needed when leading a first-generation corporate citizen; the leader is to be a teacher, and must offer his employees' advice. So, what does it require for a coach to give advice? It does not mean that he has to play the game or serve in the role, but he'd better be an expert in the game—or, in this case, business leadership.

The world is filled with coaches. Some focus on assisting ordinary folks to find purpose in their lives; others are listeners; still others emphasize experience and the need to give everyone a chance to play. Only a select few of these coaches have ever won awards, or gained champion status, but I had the great fortune as a teenager to play for a championship coach. Steve Simmons took a bunch of undersized boys from central Illinois and molded them into state champions. But what is it exactly that separates the championship coaches from the rest?

For one thing, great coaches keep things simple. Some people still cling to the idea that complicated is sophisticated. For the best results, great leaders know that nothing can replace the basics, so they spend time helping their employees excel in the fundamentals. Championship coaches also focus on creating cohesion among the stars, nonstars, and support players so that the team works together to win. Great coaches are able to motivate all of them, without exception.

You see, success comes to leaders who relentlessly teach their employees to perform their best. It follows from this that, whatever the criteria for employee development, the emphasis can only be on quality. Without a certain level of quality—to be determined by the leader—the outcome will remain uncertain. This is not to say, though, that skills will automatically translate into performance. Based on our discussion thus far, the emphasis in the Middle East has to be on developing such traits of success, performance orientation, purposefulness, and willingness to stay within organizational practices. None of these occurs naturally in an organization. It is the leader's responsibility to cultivate them within the context of the region, where the workforce largely comprises first-generation corporate employees.

It is ill-informed to think that the habits for private-sector success would have been developed prior to showing up in the workforce. In the past, government programs have raised awareness regarding the skills, behaviors, and even prescriptions for behavior that are acquired through on-the-job training. But such programs are not a panacea; nor can the private sector rely

... IN A FIRST GENERATION CORPORATE SOCIETY

solely on them. There is no getting around the leader's main responsibility—paving the way to success on his or her own.

The essence of leadership is to help others succeed—specifically your team, and in this case first-generation corporate citizens. According to this tip, you need to nurture private-sector achievement. Since each business market has a life cycle, look back in history for when others made this same transition for insights and don't ignore the different performance orientations.

TIP #3:

SPEED UP WHEN DEALING WITH THE YOUTH BULGE

Speed and youthfulness do not always make for a good combination. At sixteen years old, I received my driver's license and was obsessed with driving fast. And for youth, the consequence of speed is often recklessness. Unfortunately for my parents and their insurance bill, in my case it resulted in eleven accidents in my first two years of driving. Thank goodness my driving patterns have changed.

A similar relationship between youth and speed holds true in the workplace.

The Middle East has one of the youngest populations in the world. Thirty-four percent of the population is under the age of fourteen, and 44 percent is under twenty, compared to only 21 percent under twenty in Europe and America. This has created a "youth bulge," something that occurs when the proportion of young people distorts the population pyramid. Throughout history, the youth bulge has predictably led to social unrest or future competitive advantage.

For a period of time, this bulge is a burden on society and increases the dependency ratio as those not in the labor force are dependent on the labor force. Fortunately for the Middle East, eventually this group begins to enter the productive labor force and creates a demographic dividend in that young working-age adults comprise a disproportionate percentage of a country's population and the national economy is positively affected.

It is not only the region's workforce that is young; so is the private-sector market. Consider when some leading companies in the region were created: Zain (1983), Emirates Airline (1985), Qtel (1987), Qatar Airways (1994), Emaar Properties (1997), DP World (1999), Etihad Airlines (2004), and DU (Emirates Integrated Telecommunications Company; 2005). Actually, the modern Middle East as a whole is still very youthful given the region's ancient heritage.

So, what does this mean for business leaders in the region? Well, it means that you will be leading the youth bulge as it enters the workforce. There is no escaping this, and leading a young workforce has never been simple at the best of times. Age affects how individuals view organizational life and respond to the issues and challenges before them. For the rest of your leadership career in the Middle East, you will need to be an expert on leading a young workforce.

Leading a young workforce is significantly different from leading in a mature organization. Youthful employees are energetic, ambitious, and often idealistic. This requires leaders to roll up their sleeves and take a radically more active role in leading. A young workforce begs you to become more involved in the day-to-day workings and to provide on-the-job development, which is proven to be the most effective form of development. Additionally, leaders need to set aside traditions and give their workforce the opportunity to be ambitious (while mitigating the related risks), and they need to leverage their workforce, thinking as a racecar driver might when positioning his car up for success on the racetrack.

The youth bulge and rapid population growth means that employees are being and will be promoted beyond their capability and at a more rapid pace than is traditionally considered to be appropriate. In light of this, leaders must specialize in growing their employees' capability, confidence, and behavior in a condensed period of time and at an accelerated rate.

The markets in the Middle East are encumbered with pressures coming from a young workforce, and responsiveness to a rapidly expanding market. The question is how organizations can create opportunity from the demographic dividend.

LEARN FROM OTHERS' EXPERIENCE

A scan through workplace history highlights another era in which the youth population entered the workforce in mass. If we are to compare the US workforce in the 1970s with today's workforce in the Middle East, there are two parallel themes: a young workforce (youth bulge) and noteworthy demographic shifts.

A Dartmouth University study, for instance, found that an influx of young workers lowers the overall quality of management and the total factor of productivity, a variable that accounts for effects in total output not caused by traditionally measured inputs. A massively younger workforce means that the average age of managers drops, and this typically lowers the labor productivity per hour as they are still maturing into effectiveness in their roles.

A young workforce, logically, means that there is a higher propensity for the manager's age to drop because someone has to manage things. The Dartmouth study concluded that one of three scenarios has to unfold: there can be an increase in the span of control (the number of people that a manager manages); people who are not qualified to be managers become managers because there is no other option; or young workers become managers ahead of their time. All three of these scenarios result in the same conclusion: lower managerial quality and consequentially lower employee productivity. Given the youthfulness of the workforce in the Middle East, we risk repeating these same scenarios unless we learn from others' mistakes.

Seizing market opportunities can present significant a risk if, given the youth bulge, talent is still wanting in the organization. This is another thing with which the leader has to contend. The GCC's rapid growth has rendered the traditional "grow your own" and "promote from within" approach manifestly inadequate to meet staffing and growth needs in a timely fashion.

SPEEDING AHEAD

Let's turn our attention to applying this tip—speed up when leading the youth bulge. The key consideration arising from leading a youthful workforce and the massive youth bulge is the need for speed. The Middle East is one of the most exciting and potentially complex leadership environments in the modern world; it is the autobahn of business. Simply stated, this means that much of what works in other environments and regions needs to be reconsidered and, if applied, done so at an accelerated pace.

SPEED UP WHEN DEALING WITH THE YOUTH BULGE

These markets are encumbered with pressures stemming from a young workforce and responsiveness to a rapidly expanding market. So how are leaders to keep pace?

CHOOSE THE RIGHT APPROACH FOR LEADING IN THIS MARKET

John Chambers of Cisco says, "All of my biggest mistakes occurred because I moved too slowly." So, how do you lead with speed? Please forgive the oversimplicity of this analogy, but it does bring to life what it takes to lead the youth bulge. Think for a moment, and answer the question, what does it take to drive fast?

Not long ago, I was sitting at a standstill in Cairo traffic, once again making my way across the metropolis, and I learned a couple of things about speed. First, I learned that a Porsche is not the fastest mode of transport on the gridlocked streets. Rather, contrary to common sense, the slow-moving giant construction trucks were by far the fastest vehicle on the road, as every car was giving way to them. As soon as I realized how far we were going and how long it would take, I commented that earlier in the morning I had run this same distance in half the amount of time it would take to drive it.

What we needed was the right vehicle for the environment. It doesn't matter how fast your car is if the environment is not right for it. After first arriving in Dubai, I quickly realized that I needed to change my style of driving if I was going to survive and enjoy the roads in the United Arab Emirates

Leaders have to do the same thing by adapting to the local environment—they need to choose the right approach for their followers. In a youthful and fast-growth market, your leadership style should be open, nimble, imaginative, able to navigate ambiguity, and—most important—not restrained by heavy bureaucracy and controls. . The leadership moral here is that it is important to have the right leadership approach for the business environment.

KNOW THE ROAD

Once you've selected the right vehicle and decided on the right approach, then knowing the road should give you even more insight. This part is too often overlooked. Think of it as a commonsense approach: if the driver of a car does not know the road, he or she will be more hesitant and overly cautious.

As a leader, this means making sure your team knows your strategy (where you are heading) and plan (how you will get there), and that both you and the team know your people (those who will help you get there). I've never understood why this is difficult for leaders to understand and apply. But it is even more important in fast-growth markets that are characterized by ambiguity, complexity, rapid change, and youthfulness.

CLEAR THE ROAD

Speed bumps, congestion on the road, debris, and others' accidents all stand in the way of speed. To a business, speed bumps are organizational bureaucracy, government interference, risk aversion, protectionism, overcontrol, and even the competition. The effective leader has the capacity to circumvent or remove all of the barriers to speed so that his or her business revenue, profits, and market share can grow rapidly. If you neither clear the road nor navigate through its impediments the speed of the market will cause it to move right past you and potentially put you out of business.

PROVIDE CLARITY

A young workforce needs clear direction. Without it, employees will get distracted and try to go in every direction at once. It is your job as leader to point them in the right direction, give tips on how to get the work done, and set them free to sprint forward. But don't forget that providing clarity includes on-the-job and at-pace accountability.

In many ways, when it comes to speed, a leader is like a jockey with his horse. It is the jockey's job to keep the horse focused. Wherever the jockey looks, the horse tends to lean in that direction. Similarly, to provide clarity, as a leader you need to personally stay focused on the outcome you want to achieve. When trying to go fast, a glance off course can lead you and your team into the rails.

AVOID CRASHING

I was watching my son play a game on his PlayStation called *Grand Theft Auto*. As I sat and watched, I noticed he hadn't mastered how to drive fast. As a result, he became a cyberhazard to himself and to everyone on the road—even to those *near* the road. It's not a whole lot different for leaders who haven't mastered leadership in the context of a fast-growth market. They become like my son in *Grand Theft Auto* and me as a teenager—hazards to everyone around them. We meet people like that whenever they "crash" into us in company corridors.

One big danger about fast leadership is that when you crash at top speeds, it's a big deal! Therefore, to lead successfully in fast-growth markets, leaders must (1) have the right vehicle for the local business environment, (2) know the roadway of business, (3) remove the barriers to speed, (4) provide clarity, and (5) avoid crashing.

"ARABIZING" THE WORKFORCE

Given the implications of the youth bulge and realizing the demographic dividend, the private sector is facing the tension of deciding between importing more workers or leveraging the youthful workforce. Not long ago, on a flight between Doha and Dubai, I was seated beside the CEO of a leading company in the region, and we struck up a conversation on leading in the United Arab Emirates. As our conversation progressed, I asked this experienced CEO what he was doing to build his national workforce.

His answer startled me. "Nationalization," he said, "is nothing more than a tax to do business here in the region. Just as expats like us work to minimize the tax consequences back home in the United Kingdom or some other Western country, we also work to reduce the tax we pay in the form of nationalization." Obviously he has a mistaken perspective and is ignoring a significant part of the vision of the GCC, which is to build the capability of nationals.

The subject of nationalization has always intrigued me. It is perfectly legitimate to want to see more of one's nationals in the private sector, as many local governments keep claiming. What I find hard to comprehend is the private sector's reaction to this relatively recent initiative. In particular, the expatriate leaders have responded unenthusiastically to the idea of nationalization for the most part. But I wonder if anyone has asked them if they would be more agreeable to importing temporary talent back home—as people do in the Middle East—except as a last resort. I suspect not! Besides, the idea of a workforce built through local talent has been an intrinsic part of industry from its earliest days.

Whom did Henry Ford hire to build his model T? Why do leaders in the Middle East revolt against the standard practice of hiring local talent straight from universities and developing the employees' corporate skills, attitudes, and behaviors? The excuses from the leaders are prevalent, but not unique. Here are some I have heard:

- the demand for high salaries
- unrealistic expectations related to promotions
- high turnover rates

But what expatriate do you know who has no interest in a salary raise, has no inflated career ambitions, or will not change jobs more readily here than he or she would back home? Clearly, none of the excuses listed above is well-founded, since more than 80 percent (and probably closer to 90 percent) of the private sector in the GCC comprises expatriate employees. They are contributors to this behavior, driving up pay inflation, and reducing employee tenure.

YOUR RESPONSIBILITY

Instead of continually postponing addressing the reality of leading a youthful workforce, every leader must shoulder the responsibility to invest in building it. This is much wiser than limiting the options because of some rumors (or, possibly, past experience) and sticking with the idea that employee development is nothing but a "tax." Leaders have a golden opportunity to believe in those who join the workforce, because today those people actually believe that they can succeed. The problem is confused policies and a rapidly evolving social context.

Second, leaders need to embrace the reality and should have a short-term focus on building the youthful workforce's core capabilities for success in their organization. This may require reworking graduate/trainee programs, building managers and leaders to serve as active mentors, and adopting a patriarchal view.

Finally, leaders need to think and act for the long haul, but with a speedy mind-set. Although expatriate leaders are on time-limited contracts, and they face pressures to produce results in the short term, they should nevertheless keep the best interests of the company and the host country foremost in mind. Leaders need to make clear decisions about their workforce in the same fashion that they would "back home." They have a responsibility to build their young workforce for the future, and in the GCC this needs to include nationals.

Most experts agree that the focus needs to be on building private-sector skills across the region. Given the youth bulge and the fact that this region really is a first-generation corporate society, that makes sense. But this is not the first time that the world has met this challenge. Acting speedily would have more beneficial long-term effects than moving slowly or according to the rhythms of established markets that do not have the youth bulge or demographic dividend.

There is no doubt a certain attraction to abdicating responsibility to government programs. But the private sector needs to create the jobs and the programs that will build a local or regional workforce; the private sector needs to take the lead. While the governments can support the efforts to "Arabize" the workforce, it is up to the private sector to do it.

Now, what needs to be done? Government programs and the private sector need to invest heavily in building skills and a corporate mind-set. Since there are many success stories in the private sector across the Middle East, we should learn from them as to what sets them apart and leverage this intelligence in order to spread it across the private sector.

PROVIDE ACCOUNTABILITY

Leaders need to provide accountability for how the youth bulge is working and for achieving results, but without acting as micromanagers. As should be anticipated, a young workforce is usually inexperienced, and inexperience leads to more mistakes than are made by seasoned workers. This necessitates leaders spending time addressing quality and output while providing control—without being too controlling.

It is a bit like driving a car; the driver needs to be in control. But the faster the car goes, the more responsive the driver needs to be in order to avoid a crash. As a young driver I was obsessed with speed, yet unsafe at any speed. Just as drivers crash if they try to exert too much control, so will leaders crash if they become overcontrolling with their employees. And without accountability they will "drive all over the road." So, provide accountability to make sure they succeed.

DEVELOP TALENT, AGGRESSIVELY

If there is not enough talent to meet the demands of an organization's explosive and continued growth, then the organization has no choice but to invest in the development of such talent. Hiring from other companies is always an option, but in the end that will create a talent bubble and pay inflation, which is an economic risk for the future of the company and the country as a whole. Many organizations put off employee development because they fear becoming a talent factory that others might hire from. Of course, this is a risk, but think of the alternative; it is much riskier not to have talent in place.

ALLOW EXPOSURE

A commonality among successful leaders is that they have been exposed to possible future challenges and role requirements long before they assume their leadership roles. Unfortunately, this only occurs by happenstance, except on rare occasions when they have had the guidance of a good mentor. People who move up need role models who provide a preview of the future reality.

GUIDANCE

I use the word *guidance* to denote the active part of leading a youthful workforce. While training programs are important, their value will never surpass that of a leader making a serious effort to guide another. Leaders who are serious about growing their employees will roll up their sleeves for the tougher task of teaching and helping them acquire the mind-set, skills, and behavior needed. This effort not only grows employees for the future but also improves the quality of the present.

SUPPORT

Do not abandon your employees once you hire them, as often happens. Just because you have recruited them and they have joined your organization does not mean that they do not still need support. Remember that you are their source of inspiration and encouragement; you are the coach they learn from as you create opportunities for them to improve their performance. This is not a job only for a human resources department; it is every leader's responsibility and privilege to cultivate others.

Leading a young workforce is one of the most challenging assignments that many leaders ever face, because it requires them to set aside many existing leadership practices to which they've become too accustomed, and to adopt more hands-on development that is buoyed with on-the-job development rather than just relying on training.

Leaders need to put on their driving gloves and be ready for all of the speed and excitement that a youthful market and workforce brings. When I think of the GCC, I think of speed; it is the picture of a fast-growth market. We know that there are risks associated with going fast. For example, in the midst of fast growth, many employers promote employees beyond their capabilities at a pace that is traditionally not considered appropriate.

LIKE A FATHER RAISES A SON

Recently, after I gave the keynote address at the Middle East Business Leaders Summit, a seasoned CEO asked me, "How do you build responsibility into future leaders?" This is a question that I'm frequently asked. If you are like most leaders, you may have an opinion on how to grow leaders yet you remain inquisitive about what you could be doing better. So let's take a look at this very important topic of growing leaders in a region that is gripped by a youth bulge.

The answer lies in the heart of Arab tradition, where the father is a paramount figure in the life and development of a son.

He is the symbol of authority and the chief of guidance, being actively involved in the son's upbringing.

Leaders can be formed in similar fashion. Simply taking an active role in the growth of employees—who are, of course, not children—will ensure that they are prepared for the work it will take to meet the challenges ahead.

Arab life is rife with practical leadership development examples—consider the *majlis*, where the sons sit among adult men and are expected to behave like adults, usually not speaking but sitting quietly at the side listening to the grown-ups' conversation. Amazingly, the children rarely squirm or fidget, moving only to offer hospitality or when they are instructed to do so. In the Bedouin tradition, children assumed adult responsibilities at an early age—tending goats, collecting firewood, and doing household chores. Even in the more urban environments, fathers brought their sons to the shop, where the boys learned the commercial skills of trade.

H. H. Sheikh Mohammed bin Rashid Al Maktoum, prime minister of the United Arab Emirates and ruler of Dubai, is a modern-day example of a father raising a son and a leader raising a leader. Instead of relying exclusively on the formal education and training that his son H. H. Sheikh Hamdan bin Mohammed Al Maktoum received from the United Kingdom's Royal Military Academy Sandhurst, where the sons of royalty regularly go for advanced military training and leadership preparation, Sheikh Mohammed created a day-to-day environment in which his son could learn to lead. Clearly, education means more than what takes place via formal schooling. Schools are designed to meet academic requirements, but it is the family that teaches values, social conscience, and leader-like behavior.

SPEED UP WHEN DEALING WITH THE YOUTH BULGE

Sheikh Hamdan confesses that his father is his tutor in life. He continues to learn from him and looks to him a guiding star regarding many strategic issues, much like Sheikh Mohammed did with his father, Sheikh Rashid bin Saeed Al Maktoum.

So, what can we learn from the practice of raising a son that we can apply in the corporate world to raise leaders? Becoming a leader is more than receiving a promotion and taking a training course. Successful preparation requires exposure, guidance, opportunity, and support.

Growing a leader in the way a father raises a son (or daughter) is a greatly improved approach to the sink-or-swim or promotion-and-training-course approach. In addition to building skill and behavior, it psychologically prepares the leader for the future while equipping him or her to take advantage of the opportunities of the future.

The Middle East is in a very unique position because of the imbalance of the age of its population. It is working against time and tradition, because local managers and leaders are needed in a shorter time frame than is typically required to develop the expected level of capability in the workforce. As a result, heavy investment is needed in growing leaders for the future. Learn from the "fatherly" role models, and take active responsibility in building future leaders.

TIP #4:

RECEIVE THE SOUL WHILE PERCEIVING THE APPEARANCE

It is easy to be distracted by the glitz, glamour, and seemingly Western ways that appear evident on the surface in the Middle East. For that matter, anyone from anywhere is likely to bump into a subset of people, traditions, and values from his or her home culture. But don't waltz in and take these appearances at face value. Just because they're familiar does not mean they are similar. If you don't look below the surface, you'll miss the soul of the society.

Many people are tricked by similarities and make false conclusions based on them. Several years ago, my parents experienced this firsthand during their first visit to the Middle East. Prior to that trip, they were worried about culture shock; I reassured and even warned them that they would be more surprised by what appeared as familiar. Upon arriving, they quickly noted many of the same restaurants and shops they had in their hometown in the middle of America. My dad even commented, "You live closer to more American shops and restaurants than I do, and I live there."

This observation is merited on first glance, but deeper investigation reveals that more than two hundred nationalities call the region home. And any one of them can make similar claims to my parents if in the right areas. There is no question that globalization is, at least on the surface, changing the appearance of the region's culture and dressing it in things that bare similarity to most anyone's home environment.

With respect to leading, though, it is important to look beyond the surface similarities to your homeland and to see the true soul of the local culture, which remains Arab. As in any society, connecting with it comes from receiving its soul, which in this case is steeped in Pharaonic, Phoenician, Bedouin, and Islamic traditions.

THE PHARAOHS

The Middle East has a complex history. Centuries-old relics from ancient Egyptian dynasties still exist in modern Arabia, as does the related hierarchy of those dynasties. These factors still influence the contemporary social, family, and business structures in the region. There remains a reverential designation for the ruler; leadership titles command respect. The prevailing structure of the leader and the led in this region still finds its genesis in the model of the Pharaoh, at a time when there was a supreme leader and the positional heritage was passed from one generation to the next through the sons.

Hopefully we have advanced beyond the negative aspects of that era, beyond ill-advised attempts to emulate a Pharaoh more interested in building monuments to himself than in creating a future for his people.

THE PHOENICIANS

Long before the Silk Road cut through the region, the Phoenicians pioneered trade as a confederation of maritime traders. Lacking many natural resources other than the cedars of Lebanon, they founded trading ports all around the Mediterranean. Their contribution expanded beyond trade; among other accomplishments, they created what we know today as the alphabet. But they are still known for their talent as traders, a bedrock feature of the Arab business mentality.

THE BEDOUINS

Bedouins have their own unique history and social systems, based on complicated social allegiances. This is clear from one of their sayings: "I against my brother, my brothers and I against my cousins, my cousins and I against strangers." Bedouin social structures range from the nuclear family to the broader family and on to the tribe. The glue of the family is the hierarchy of sons. Bedouin culture reinforces this hierarchy with a strong honor code, the set of rules or ethical principles that govern a community and define what constitutes honorable behavior within that community.

The value of an honor code depends on the notion that people (at least within the community) can be trusted to act honorably. It also embraces abstract concepts like worthiness and respectability, both of which affect social standing and self-evaluation. Individuals (or corporate bodies) are assigned worth and stature based on the harmony of their actions within this specific code of honor.

While each of these cultures—Pharaonic, Phoenician, and Bedouin—is rooted in distinct historical eras and different, if geographically close, lands, the modern Middle East business environment is influenced by them all. Their importance in our understanding the soul of Middle Eastern society cannot be emphasized enough.

THE WAY OF LIFE

To understand the business culture of the Middle East, and thus to provide leadership, you cannot discount the influence of Islam. I am speaking not simply of local mosque attendance but of Islam as the cultural underpinning of society. Just as the West has been shaped by the practice of Christianity over centuries, the Middle East has become what it is largely through the influence of Islam.

Islam does not concern itself merely with the spiritual aspects of life; it is an entire ethos that embraces the spiritual, moral, social, educational, and economic aspects of life. Furthermore, it does not separate the religious from state authority in the way done in the West. It is a religion of practice that is publicly visible, not only a private inner belief. For this reason, it influences the business environment throughout the Middle East, through a communal system of beliefs that imposes a strict ritual, moral code, and dictates accepted practices and relationships within a narrowly defined tradition. Leaders have to understand the broader impact of this form of religion on members of Arabic society.

A beauty of this culture is the understanding, tolerant, and respectful character that distinguishes its people. Despite the stereotype of the region spread by international news outlets, in reality the market understands that many, if not most, expatriates have value systems and practices that differ from those of the local culture. While these values and practices may not be to their own personal liking, locals are nevertheless tolerant of them. Of course they try to limit their personal involvement in behavior frowned on in their own culture, but they understand others' backgrounds and tolerate their actions. You will find a tremendous amount of respect built into the workings of Arab society.

The inhabitants of Middle Eastern countries are proud of their traditions, and they anchor their business culture in them. Furthermore, local leaders, who also reflect the regional cultural values, have a strong influence on the local community. The result is a mindset that seeks ways to embrace progress while maintaining a respect for tradition.

EXHIBIT WORKPLACE INTELLIGENCE

So how can you as a leader master this unique challenge? First, you need to be empathic; employees have had incredibly different life experiences than you have had. As a leader, you should look for and try to find the points of connection. In this economy, empathy is very important for motivating a team, and you won't have it if you don't walk in their shoes a bit and see life from their perspective.

The faster you as a leader are able to understand issues from other viewpoints and build a climate of trust, the deeper the impact on performance will be. When working with expatriates, leaders need to develop the ability to understand others' mental states and, more importantly, what underlies their behavior.

This is workplace intelligence; it is based upon the ability to understand and sense where others are coming from and build a climate a trust.

Second, you need to understand and accept the fact that the foundational soul of the Middle East is Islamic, for the majority. Successful leaders do not spend their time trying to fight this fact or even work around it. Rather, they accept it and respect what it means for the region. Perhaps the most difficult part is to negotiate the plethora of religious subsets across society. Mastery in receiving the soul while perceiving the appearance comes from a combination of empathy, acceptance, and tolerance.

CULTURAL CONNOISSEUR

In the past, many companies have selected foreigners with limited experience to head their operations in the Middle East. While these leaders have cognitively known that they should adapt their leadership and management styles to fit the preferences of the local culture, they have still applied historical models of leadership and turned to past examples of best practice.

Naturally, this approach has not yielded the desired result, because it does not reflect the cultural and structural realities of an emerging economy. Many significant changes in the market—the increasing cultural diversity of the labor force, globalization, organizational restructuring, and international mergers and acquisitions—make it nearly impossible to smoothly transfer Western motivational approaches and managerial practices across cultures without taking into consideration the interactions of individual differences and contextual factors. It is time that leaders shift away from the notion of importing leadership and discover who their workforce is, embracing a hybrid leadership skill set that will lead to success.

Leaders must discover the elements that shape a workforce and how it performs, acknowledging that the workforce has acceptable differences from their own background and previous experience. In doing so, they will be able to begin the journey to appreciate their employees for who they are and gain their trust—in short, to lead. A bridge must be built between the workforce and the leaders, who, as highlighted in my first tip, should adapt their leadership style to fit the demands and needs of the local workforce while focusing on their organization's strategic vision and goals.

Successfully leading in the Middle East is like acquiring a taste for foreign cuisine. It begins with discovering that different foods have different tastes, smells, textures, and so on. We may know this intuitively, but experiencing it is what creates real understanding and awareness. This process is always exciting, even if discovering the background of a dish we are eating may sometimes unnerve us. Over time, a "foodie" will become acquainted with the differences and begin to appreciate the variations between regional specialties. Eventually, taste buds adapt to the flavors of the local cuisine. Just as many people are not able to appreciate any tastes that differ from those in their home culture, many people in leadership positions simply do not acquire an understanding of the local workforce, and as a result do not maximize their leadership impact.

That first *meze*, when the Middle East changed the course of my life, left an unforgettable impression on me. Sitting on the table with at least a dozen Lebanese who were very proud of their food was definitely a process of discovery, as they piled heaps of food onto my plate that I could not even pronounce the name of and stuck things straight into my mouth. I must admit that at first I was very unfamiliar with and even unsure of the food.

They told me we were going to have "wings." I pictured in my mind typical buffalo wings from BW3, a place back home famous for their wings. What appeared next was far from what I was expecting; what were called wings were more like tiny birds. I watched to see what the host did; he stuck it right in his mouth and ate away, so I did the same. Then, as the tiny bones crunched between my teeth, all I could hear was my mom's voice: "Don't swallow the chicken bones, you might choke." With those words ringing in my head, my throat started to close, and I wished I were eating wings from BW3.

Leading is not much different from this encounter with a new food. At first other cultures are intriguing and distinct, confusing and even weird, but after time we become used to them. Just as I yearned for BW3, leaders also wish to be able to lead the way they did back at home, with people they understand. But over time, what at first seemed strange becomes second nature; then you are on your path to becoming a cultural connoisseur and leadership success.

Organizational leaders need to explore their new environment and identify the elements that define their employees' background and create the optimal operational environment needed to propel employee performance. To accomplish this, leaders need to be able to answer the question "Who is the Middle Eastern workforce?"

Middle Eastern economies are undergoing major structural, demographic, and socioeconomic changes as the populations in these countries experience unmatched population growth, rapid economic expansion, and integration into the global economy.

RECEIVE THE SOUL WHILE PERCEIVING THE APPEARANCE

This is a challenging topic for most leaders, who come from monocultural societies and rarely have lived in a "new" city, which draws its workforce and residents from all over the world. Skill in balancing appearance and the soul of the culture is what creates the ability to drive business into and across multiple markets. Experience shows that expatriates (Western and from developing countries) tend to settle into subsets of society that are familiar to them, and as a result draw flawed conclusions about the markets and their employees, based on limited understanding.

Is your leadership based upon what feels familiar to you? Or are you driving at the soul of the society, the market, and your employees?

Most externally exposed leaders understand that conducting business in the Middle East is going to be different from conducting business outside the region. They anticipate that the market will have its own rhythms, that consumers may have different buying patterns and preferences, and that leaders may have some difficulty interpreting government policies and practices. Beyond investing in consumer market data and reading guidebooks on local culture, leaders need to invest in understanding who the workforce is, acting as a connoisseur. Your ability to maximize employee discretionary effort and, thus, business success depends on how well you as a leader understand the differences in your workforce is different, and how you work from that understanding to engage it to perform.

TIP #5:

REMEMBER THAT THE FUTURE IS NOT MEASURED BY THE QUARTER

Businesses in the Middle East measure success by the fulfillment of a vision, not by the quarterly report, as Wall Street routinely does. Thus, at times work moves at warp speed, and at other times it may seem to crawl a snail's pace. Leaders have to understand and match these rhythms.

Fulfillment of a vision and the relentless pressure for quarterly results do not always unite. The vision of businesses in the Middle East reaches beyond common financial measures such as earnings before interest, taxes, depreciation, and amortization (EBITDA), diluted earnings per share (DEPS), and other fiscal metrics. I am not saying that these do not matter; they do. But for many firms, the true value is the legacy, which supersedes reporting cycles.

This is a very tough challenge for the time-weathered imported executive to understand, the cadence of whose life revolves around the quarterly cycle of earnings calls and fiscal projections. The pursuit of shareholder value simply fails as a unifying theory to produce real value in business. It turns CEOs into excellent managers of expectations, rather than tangible corporate performance.

Fortunately, in the Middle East, the ambitions many leading companies have are not limited to these time checks on the balance sheet. In this tip, I'm not suggesting that leaders abandon fiscal rigor. Rather, I'm highlighting differing views of time, comparing the infancy of time—the short-term view that a young child has—with the impact of time as a long-term perspective. In the Middle East, Western-trained executives need to look past short-term gains and quarterly results to understand time's real impact on fiscal gain. You need to think beyond your tenure with the company and value the emotional return on investment that is the owner's legacy.

WHO OWNS THE COMPANY?

Most local Middle Eastern businesses are in their first generation—owned by the founder—and still have entrepreneurial ambitions related to their future impact. Looking at family businesses in the region for a moment, we see that the founders have the same desires that founders of businesses all over the world have, which often conflict with the interests of external shareholders. The Middle East is dominated by family businesses, which make up 90 percent of the private sector and employ 75 percent of the workforce. Therefore, unless you own the family business, you're most likely leading in one.

By way of contrast, let's look at the majority of the Western businesses that we read about or aspire to be like. Pick any CEO of a publicly traded company. I'll choose Disney's CEO, Robert Iger, to illustrate my point. Does he really know his shareholders? At least nine million shares change hands daily. In the best-case scenario, he knows only a handful of shareholders, and these are most likely the institutional investors. The fact of the matter is that CEOs and other leaders do not really know who their shareholders are, have never met them, and for that matter, have never taken direction from them outside of shareholder meetings, which are minimal in their influence. In a family business, on the other hand, it is very clear who the owner is.

Now, pick any family business. Kuwait-based Al Shaya is a good example. We know who the "shareholder" is: Mohammed Al Shaya. Al Shaya, the company, is unlike Disney in that the only "shareholder" relationship is a personal one, relating to the founder. Such relationships can cause friction when expatriate leaders are imported. The metrics expatriates are used to are likely to differ, depending on the degree to which the owner is actively involved. In addition, the math and science of business measurement may vary widely from one family-owned business to the next. This is how local companies are—they have the advantage of youth, above all, but certain disadvantages, too.

FASCINATED WITH BEING BIGGER

As a young boy, like most kids, I was obsessed with the idea of getting bigger. I would measure my height almost daily, hoping to find evidence of growth. I recall my parents hearing my constant insistence that I was a "big boy." This continued into my adolescent years, when I would argue that I was adult-like. I am not, of course, comparing local businesses to a young child. On the contrary, their leaders should not shy away from aspiring to growth for their organization and to finding new ways to attain it. They have the same fascination I had when growing up—getting bigger.

The question remains, however: What do leaders mean by "bigger"? Traditionally speaking, there are key terms used to measure "bigger" in a business setting. Here are a few of the most common:

- Share price: The price of a single share of a number of saleable stocks of a company.
- P/E (price-to-earning ratio): The price paid for a share of a company relative to the annual net income or profit earned by the company per share.
- EBITDA: Earnings before interest, taxes, depreciation, and amortization.
- Top-line growth: The annual gross sales or revenue.
- Size of workforce: How many employees a company has.
- Market share: Percentage of a market accounted for by a specific company.

While these are universal business measurements, given the reality that family businesses account for 90 percent of the private sector in the Middle East, it is important to understand what "getting bigger" means for a family business.

BIGGER

Essentially, growth means increased shareholder value. But the real question is, does "growth" refer to the value of the shares or what brings value to the shareholder? To family business owners, the latter is more common. Based upon my conversations with some of the leading Middle Eastern merchant families, the idea is to get bigger and to have more, which translates into more locations, top-line revenue, and employees.

There is a fascination across the Middle East, perhaps bordering on an obsession, with being bigger. Every day there is a new story of the "biggest." Consider the following examples; the Middle East

- is home to the tallest tower in the world (and a bigger one is being planned)
- is set to see the fastest growth in the world until 2015, and possibly beyond
- has the biggest order book for jumbo jets
- has the world's largest reclamation projects
- has the world's biggest supply of oil and natural gas
- possesses some of the largest sovereign wealth funds

The list goes on. There is an inherent fascination with big, not only in the local Middle Eastern businesses but also in the region's multinational firms. As an example, a technology firm is no longer satisfied with double-digit growth year on year; they are now striving to grow at two times the rate of the market. Or consider the global retailer that opened its first store here; within twelve months it was not only their fastest-growing store but had become the biggest of their 112 stores around the world.

DELIVER RAPID AND SUSTAINABLE GROWTH

Ordinary rates of growth are often connected to market growth, modeling the idea that "if the water in the harbor rises, so do the boats." But rapid growth requires a source that is not driven exclusively by external factors.

Real growth, therefore, requires momentum. It is one thing to grow on the back of governmental infrastructure investments or even based upon additional input, but rapid growth depends on the ability to produce surplus value.

As a criterion of competitive growth, surplus value stands for the difference between returns and costs, connecting profitability with productivity. It refers roughly to the new value created by workers that is in excess of their own labor cost, thus creating the fuel for greater growth.

If an organization can extract more from its asset base without increasing input of resources, then it will be in a position to produce rapid growth. Rapid-growth leaders decouple their growth rate from payroll and other expenses. Their output outgrows their input, making them more competitive compared to their peers and realizing the productivity needed for growth that is not based on external factors.

A defining characteristic of the current business climate is that most people cannot recognize rapid growth solutions without help. Every senior executive must provide his or her people and teams with systems that help them to comprehend the potential value they need to create, and then to craft and implement these solutions in a scalable fashion. When leaders can help their people understand how they can deliver the future performance of the firm, the way they lead becomes a critical component of the value of the business and a key source of sustainable, scalable competitive advantage.

HEEDING THE RISKS

The risk associated with rapid growth comes when leaders gravitate to a cost-conscious mindset. Cost leadership is typically

REMEMBER THAT THE FUTURE IS NOT MEASURED...

about stripping out cost and growing the profit line by reducing expenditures. Capturing value is about managing cost in a way that supports rapid growth. This is a fundamental shift in organizational mindset and leadership practice: from rewarding cutting to celebrating improvements that support growth.

Companies that aren't afraid to take calculated risks can grow rapidly. The key here is "calculated." These companies' owners weigh their options, decide on a course of action, and implement it, even though there may be risk involved. While this approach doesn't always pay off, it can have far-reaching rewards. Neglecting to properly calculate risk, on the other hand, is typical of companies that fail; they jump in too fast without paying attention to the potential consequences.

While cost-cutting is seen as a sure bet, focusing on value creation requires a deeper level of business acumen and intuition. Since the rapid-growth agenda entails value creation, leaders have to reach the maximum growth rate they can sustain without relying on undue financial leverage. This type of value creation comes from continually reviewing current strategies to ensure they are still valid within the changing business environment. The trap of yesterday's activities can easily come at the expense of tomorrow's value. The crux of creating value comes through maximizing the way that employees work. Imagine the impact of a 5 percent increase in employee productivity. The top-line impact would be marvelous, while also making an almost direct contribution to the bottom line. Improving employee productivity requires setting challenging objectives that reflect key strategic medium- and longer-term priorities for the organization.

Creating surplus value is also the mechanism to drive productivity upward. It focuses an organization, fostering a higher level of thinking about achieving output. Productivity is often held captive by the way that work has been done and the way that leaders have led. Typically, organizations measure progress against how the organization has performed in the previous month, quarter, or year rather than against the potential that could be realized. Is it worth celebrating doing 10 percent better than was done in the past, if the potential to do 30 percent better exists?

All in all, the Middle East has some advantages over more established American and European rivals. While capital costs are similar around the world, Naguib Sawiris, chairman of Egypt's Orascom Telecom Holdings, says total operating expenses in the Middle East are perhaps a tenth of what they are in Britain or France, thanks to the cheaper cost of employing engineers and salespeople. Sawiris tellingly adds that the killer edge, the real advantage, is growth. In the past decade, Sawiris's operations added subscribers at the rate of over 100 percent per year.

Rapid-growth leadership refocuses attention on maximizing productivity, using regular managerial productivity analysis to make a shift in productivity output through the employees. In this way, leaders can leverage employee input to grow productivity per hour and improve organizational competitiveness, and optimize productivity as a ratio of what is produced (serviced) to what is required to produce it.

Multinational companies who are striving to grow in the Middle East are also looking for top-line revenue growth and market share as their primary measurement of success. For many, their chief focus is a revenue contribution to their balance sheet, rather than a fixation on other measures. Growth is at the forefront of their strategy, yet they are shackled with the quarterly mentality.

DELIVER RAPID AND SUSTAINABLE GROWTH

The Middle East is laden with ambiguity in business and a lack of clarity in the workforce. This partly results from an inability to understand how family businesses measure success, and to recognize the different business rhythms. The Middle East business environment is leader-centric, as we saw. The workforce looks to its leaders to lessen this ambiguity and to give direction. In some way, leaders play the role of helmsmen on the open sea—you know, the people who navigate through unclear, ever-changing waters. The capacity to navigate the ambiguities of fast-changing local environments and quickly respond to the needs of the market remains as critical as ever.

So what should leaders do to understand and match regional rhythms?

<u>Align Motives</u>

This is all about gaining sufficient appreciation of what best drives your business. Is it impact and legacy, as it is with many local businesses? Or is it quick fiscal results? Understanding motive in a family business can be very challenging for expatriate leaders. On the other hand, multinational corporations may speak of impact and legacy, but they usually expand based upon the hope of quick fiscal results.

As I've pointed out above, when you talk to family businesses, you regularly hear the refrain "We want to grow." But are your present financial metrics for growth (return on investment, market share, and so on) appropriate for this desire? Top-line revenue growth typically encapsulates the purpose of a family business. In the Middle East, however, profit is not measured as ruthlessly as it is in Western organizations.

Another metric is head count—the size of the workforce. Owners take pride in how many people they employ. Maybe this comes from the tribal or "big" family mentality. In the end, this is more than a metric for bragging. What would shame a Middle Eastern business owner is the prospect of not being able to provide for his employees' families if he let them go.

A friend of mine who was a consultant working in Egypt with a large company of seven thousand employees told the chairman, "You should be operating with five thousand employees. You should do our 'downsizing with dignity' program."

The chairman respectfully replied, "Tell me more about your program." So my friend shared the details with him. He ended the meeting confident that he would get the work, since the chairman told him, "Send me your proposal."

That night we spoke, and I remember telling him with a slight chuckle, "They're never going to buy this program."

"Why not?" he asked.

"Do you know the two questions the chairman's friends ask him?" I responded. " 'What's your turnover? and 'How many employees do you have?'"

If the chairman cut two thousand employees from his workforce, he would be reducing his honor, the recognition that he had seven thousand employees, so he could boost his profit margin. My friend would be putting him in a position where he had to tell his friends, "I have reduced my number of employees to five thousand, but I'm actually making a lot more at the end of the month." Would he be saying that his operation was more successful? Only "hearing" that he reduced his headcount, everyone would ask him, "Wow, so what's wrong with your business?"

The chairman already had enough wealth accumulated to last for generations. He had his name on the building. Despite his high station in life, he would feel ashamed of not having a workforce equal to it.

Clarify Desired Outcomes

When you align the motives, the desired outcomes become clear. It is important to have absolute clarity (understanding the other views) on whether the desired outcome is short-term results, long-term ambitions, or a combination. What are the outcomes being spoken of by the owner/board?

Role ambiguity exists due to a lack of clarity about what is expected from the leader. Since role ambiguity is especially common for expatriates, given their new work environment, the assumptions they enter the workforce with, and questions arising about the way work is evaluated, the scope of their responsibilities, and performance expectations, leaders need to be aware of this and seek clarity.

Of course, no business is in business to lose money. But actions need to be based upon what is meant by what is said, not just what is said. Many CEOs have gotten into trouble by hearing what they thought was said and not realizing that the owner/board intended a different meaning. The operating model needs to be implemented according to the desired outcomes. Is your operating model and actions in line with the desired outcomes?

It is hardly surprising that business outcome expectations should bring on a tension for business leaders in the Middle East. Successful leaders should have enough understanding of the situation to balance both the short-term and long-term perspectives while delivering according to the business owner's ambitions.

INTERPRETATION OF NOW

A fundamental difference in views is the "age" of time. In the West (specifically, in the recently developed parts of the West like modern Europe, Australia, and the United States), time is an "infant," whereas in the Middle East, time is a "seasoned adult." The idea is that the concept of time in a country or region is related to the age of that country or region—just as to a child, time holds a different value than it does for an adult. A small child can only see the present moment—what is happening now—while an adult learns a new set of standards for what is and is not acceptable in the passage of time.

If you say to a three-year-old child that something will happen in one month, that will seem like forever. One month equals 1/36th of the child's life, but to a fifty-five-year-old adult, one month equals 1/660th. The result is that the child and the adult have very different perspectives on time. The United States is just over 230 years old, whereas the Arab world is thousands of years old, and this influences the cultures' different views of time.

Another shaper of time is the phrase "Insha'Allah"—literally, "If God wills." This can be a simple statement of faith in God's willingness, in its purity, or a form of words covering the strong possibility of inaction, or even, when negatively used, can hedge apparently agreed-on courses of action. There is a strong belief in the Middle East that since time is only in God's hands, a mere human cannot be assured what will happen in the future, or control time. This idea has to be understood, as it is the heartbeat of the rhythm of life here. In parts of the Middle East, it affects how planning is carried out. When outsiders hear "Insha'Allah," they often wonder if the speaker is making excuses, or really means it. Typically, people who use this phrase are genuinely stating a belief, but this phrase can be abused as well.

Remember that the Future is not Measured...

Another concept that foreigners struggle with is *bukrah*, implying "tomorrow." Time in the West is most often seen as definite, whereas in the Arab world time has indefinite characteristics. If it is Monday, and a Westerner says tomorrow, he literally means Tuesday. He is taking time to mean something definite.

In the Arab world, *bukrah* combined with "Insha'Allah" would in practical terms mean "in the coming future" rather than precisely "the next day." Time is handled with respect for Allah, and therefore man cannot make time definite. It is important to attach Arab cultural meaning to these phrases, not exact Western interpretations.

These concepts of time have an impact on how business is conducted, but more than that they have real impact on how to manage in the Arab world. A leader has the responsibility to understand and adapt to the principles of the region if he wants to maximize his leadership potential.

Keep in mind the important historical fact that Western business models, which developed their leadership models in the postwar period, have roots in military strategizing. I mention this to highlight the mechanistic thinking behind them. They tend to be highly structured according to formalized rules and procedures. Western corporations are geared for short-term quarterly financial objectives and stock performance, while companies in the Middle East, focus on providing for future generations to come. Organizational members in more collectivistic cultures—where strong, cohesive groups take precedence over individuals—tend to attach their commitment to long-term goals.

Who can deny the excitement of growth? As you can see, though, it can be quite dangerous. If I had retained my childhood fascination with getting bigger, perhaps I would have had a heart attack, because to an adult bigger can only mean overweight, out of shape, inviting the bundle of ailments that come with this. In boom times, getting bigger is often an illusion that tells us nothing wiser than that we are better because we are bigger. When the music stops and the bills pile up, bigger will mean larger and perfectly avoidable problems. So be careful what you wish for; you may just get it.

A vision for growth, getting bigger, is the metronome of business in the Middle East. Owners can pick a beat for business that is different from the Wall Street analysts and investor-controlled boardrooms. Family business is the reality of the Middle East; we even have family-run cities and countries. Therefore, we can deliver rapid, yet sustainable, growth.

TIP #6:

ASK, "FATHER, MAY I?"

In this society, the father is the central figure and wields a great amount of authority. The traditional Arab family has a healthy respect and reverential fear of the father, looking to him for leadership. This patriarchal orientation heightens the tendency to be more leader-centric in the organization as well. The patriarch in the family understands that he has the responsibility for his family or tribe, and he does not take it lightly. As such, he is the decision maker for the group. The fundamental matrix of an Arab organization is hierarchical and consultative, representing in some ways a facsimile of the family structures in the region. Family members are still asked for feedback and opinion, but the father retains the decision-making power.

Legitimate authority rests ultimately on the apparently absolute power of the sheikh or king, who nonetheless must take account of tribal opinion in all his decisions. The Bedouin influence, with its emphasis on a patriarchal family structure, can be seen in the structure of organizations with top-down authority as the norm.

One downside of this model is the natural tendency to mimic the perception of the Pharaonic "great man" acting alone. At first glance the fiber of the society is rich with Great Men. This starts all the way back with the pharaohs, then the prophets, even the father in each family. So the natural product is to try to mimic this idea in the corporate offices.

Of course, this is an errant view. Looking deeper into history, you see the missing element—the advisers. Every one of those men relied heavily upon personal advisers or people of wisdom. The business community would be wise to look to the role of the adviser to bring a greater degree of wisdom.

LEADER-CENTRIC

In the Middle East employees' understanding of workplace practices comes from the historical dominance of the family business and the centrality of the paternalistic culture. Therefore, the workforce has a leader-centric mentality. The workforce is designed around the top position in the organization, and from this approach creates a centralized approach to providing direction, making decisions, and applying control. On the other hand, Western multinationals tend to be employee-centric; the organization recognizes the preeminence of the employee and shares responsibility and accountability with, delegates authority to, and includes the views of the employees.

When it comes to leading the workforce, the leader-centric style is an area of friction between non-native leadership theories and practical application. The Western approach is believed to "free" employees by including them in the decision-making process, but in reality that approach conflicts with Middle Eastern culture. Leaders in this region need to appreciate the differences between employee-centric and leader-centric orientations and shape their approaches accordingly.

It is important not to think that one background is better than the other and fall into the dangerous pitfall of identifying one as superior to the other. Both have great value; success will only come as leaders leverage each for insights into the workforce.

THE INFLUENCE OF THE FATHER IN BUSINESS

The Middle East is rife with family businesses. This concept is so strong in the region that there are even family-run countries. The history of the family business is a critical component of how business is conducted. A westerner must be able to answer the question, "How does the concept of family business and its culture affect leadership in general?"

Even many of the mega-businesses in the region are family owned and operated. From the exterior, they look very much like international corporations, but their deep architecture and rhythms are those of a family business, the "father" is in charge. The nature of a family business tends to be more patriarchal.

For centuries, and up to today's times, the father leading has been the predominant business model in the Middle East. So most Middle Easterners have adopted the family business model, and many even import similar practices into nonfamily businesses. Because of the prevalence of family businesses in the Middle East, it is easy to understand why family business practices are used by leaders in their work, in every kind of organization. The family business is the inherited reference point for how a business is run.

IS THERE ROOM FOR AUTOCRATIC LEADERS IN TODAY'S WORLD?

Hierarchy is alive and well all over the Arab world. In the hierarchical environment, we're talking about a situation in which the father still takes precedence in the family. Whether we agree with or like this is really immaterial—it's the reality in the Middle East. Family businesses are hierarchical, and are not about to give up that hierarchy. So the question comes back to us: Do we fight hierarchy or do we try and make it the best it can possibly be?

In the Arab home, it is common to have centralized power; similarly the influence on the patriarchal family structure can be seen in the structure of organizations in which top-down authority is the norm. The natural, but mistaken, outcome of centralized power is control, and this controlling mentality can limit a leader's ultimate influence and success. The tight locus of control and power that is experienced in the business context comes from mimicking the home style of leadership. To lead in the Middle East, it is essential to understand where these patterns come from and why they exist; this understanding is essential to success.

The Middle East experienced some pretty wild activity with uprisings against long-established and deeply embedded leaders. Clearly having reached the point of frustration, and with a little bit of confidence, millions of people took to the streets demanding that many of their governmental leaders step down. We are past the point of caution, as this leadership dilemma has reached

ASK, "FATHER, MAY I?"

historic magnitude and all business leaders need to understand what it means for them. As I have watched this unique leader-follower combustion, I have wondered, will the latest casualty of the political uprisings be the demise of autocratic leadership?

The Hay Group's research has found that the predominant style of leadership in the region is command and control. While many people argue that this needs to change, including Hay Group, we need to be realistic about the business life cycle and the style of business in the region. Ninety percent of the companies are family businesses, and the majority in the workforce is comfortable with the clarity and strength coming from autocratic leadership in a hierarchical environment. Instead of fighting this approach, leaders need to be realistic and work to make it the best it can be.

Leadership scholars say that autocratic leadership is the least desirable style when it comes to building trusting relationships, because they hypothesize that when one person is in complete control, no one is permitted to make any suggestions or offer any opinions, no matter how it may benefit the group. In other words, autocratic leadership equals command and control. But this is an incomplete understanding. Autocratic leadership can simply and most accurately be translated as "a person with unlimited power or authority."

Although many people immediately assume and even argue that autocratic leadership is a bad style and should not be used, is it really that bad? Of course it is when it takes the extreme form of dictatorship. But we need to be careful not to confuse autocratic leadership with totalitarianism. In these extreme instances, the leader does not involve others in the decision-making process, and may even resort to threats, manipulation, or even force to accomplish his or her goals.

But not all autocratic leaders are bad. We can look across the Middle East and see excellent examples of the collective benefits of autocratic leadership. In reality, most family businesses rely on the autocratic style of leading. And many employees in the region prefer this style given their own patriarchal or hierarchical societal backgrounds. In the workplace there are some real benefits of an autocratic style, especially in ambiguous, volatile, uncertain, and rapidly changing markets. When operating conditions call for urgent action, the autocratic style of leadership may be the best one to enact.

The *majlis* is a central part of the cultural history of the Middle East. Literally, it is a meeting room in a sheikh's or other leader's home. In reality, it is more than the actual room where guests congregate; traditionally it represents the gathering of advisers and guests to discuss issues, air problems, and make decisions. It is the forum for consultation and the building of consensus. The leader still holds positional authority—autocracy—but he listens and takes on board the opinions of those being led.

While this tradition that spans centuries is practiced less frequently, only a few families still host a daily *majlis*, but the spirit of it is still very much alive. The art of consultation is very much in the fiber of regional leadership, and in what I call a "virtual" *majlis* it is common for the patriarch to spend time on the phone calling up each adviser and stakeholder, asking each the same question and seeking their input. This is very frustrating for Western leaders who think they were brought in with some authority. Repeatedly I hear it said, "I don't think my boss trusts me." When I ask, "Why do you feel this?" the answer is often, "He calls my peers, direct reports, his friends and asks all of them same question." Consultation and seeking

ASK, "FATHER, MAY I?"

a broad range of opinions is very much a part of autocratic leadership in the Middle East and is in keeping with the spirit of the *majlis*.

So, if in some instances autocratic leadership is brilliant and in others it is dreadful, what makes the difference?

The leader's motive is the core indicator as to how autocratic leadership will be exhibited; in other words, is the leader acting for the betterment of all or for the fulfillment of his or her ideal at all costs? This danger is evidenced when a leader projects that he or she knows what is best for everyone else even when the masses speak with a unified contrarian voice. The litmus test for motive comes down to "self, or others?"

The second difference between autocratic leadership being brilliant or dreadful is whether the leader is aligning his or her style with the needs of the moment, environment, and followers. Notably, many individuals have already worked for an autocratic leader and therefore have little trouble adapting to that style. Many employees who are working in the private sector for the first time prefer an autocratic style and like the clarity that comes with being told exactly what to do. There is a preference for a clear and strong approach to leadership, but not for a dictatorial style.

The benefit of autocratic leadership is that it brings surety in this region to those being led—those who are mainly first-generation corporate citizens. When the leader comes in and asks his employees, "Hey, how do you think we ought to handle this?" it raises uncertainty. The employees begin to think, "If my boss doesn't know, we're in trouble. He's asking me what we should do!" Don't get this point wrong; when you work with more senior employees the level of directness needs to be more inclusive.

The question leaders need to be clear about is, "Am I empowering on direction or empowering on solution?" Founder-leaders like Steve Jobs give clear direction as regards to where the company is going and what it's doing, but empower their teams to figure out how to get there.

Given the prominence of the centrality of the father in the Middle East, it is advised that every leader lead with paternalistic qualities, as if leading a family, clan, or tribe. A leader should act in a protective, supportive, and responsible way toward those being led, and think first of the nature of the group that is being led and what he or she desires to accomplish rather than the actual position being occupied.

LEADERS IN NAME ONLY

Is leadership simply about having a position? Or is there more to it?

Many who occupy positions of leadership and think or act as if, because they hold these positions, they are leaders. But are they really? They might just be LINOs—leaders in name only.

A LINO is the de facto leader since he or she holds the respected position. But in reality a LINO is far from being a practicing leader—thus "in name only." Have you every met a LINO? Or, worse yet, worked for one? Surely we all have had LINO interactions during our working careers. But today's real question goes to you—are *you* a LINO? This past year has been a year of awakening for business executives, who have been bravely asking, "Are my leaders any good?" Each time I am asked this, I pause and probe the inquiry. It seems that executive leaders in the region have real concerns about the quality of the other leaders in their organization. We can conclude that they are worried that they have the dreaded LINOs.

The idea of a LINO raises a potential weakness of the autocratic style. It is acceptable for the patriarch to act as an autocrat given his role and ownership. Additionally, as has been pointed out, the patriarch is most likely consultative and thinking about what is best for all. But when LINOs, even as middle and frontline managers, begin to act as autocrats it is not acceptable. They have a role to play, and it needs to be played as a caring patriarch, not a dictator.

So why do employees follow a leader—only because of his or her position? Being a LINO is the least desirable of the five reasons why people follow leaders:

Because of Your Position
People follow leaders because they have to until they have an opportunity not to. Just because you hold a leadership position does not mean you are a leader in that seat. During the revolutions in northern Africa, the people took to the streets to get rid of their leaders. In the corporate world, employees make this decision daily with their feet by changing employers to get a new (and hopefully better) manager. Employees who have a LINO typically perform at the bare minimum to sustain their role until they cannot take it anymore. Having a title or position does not equate with being a leader.

Because of the Relationship
Sometimes people follow leaders because they like them. So if you are a likeable person, you have a decent chance that people will follow you or at least want to be with you. But are you leading them? Without a doubt, personality is an asset for a leader. But if you are relying solely on your personality for your leadership effectiveness, you are in real danger when it comes to

being able to sustain this and, most important, deliver results for your organization.

Because of the Results You Produce

People like to follow leaders who produce results and do great things for the organization. Leaders gain credibility, and people begin to follow because of what they have done for the organization. Everyone likes to be on a winning team. And winners have a strong cadre of followers, but what happens when the winning stops? Many fans stop cheering and cease to attend the games, and some fair-weather fans even switch teams; employees can, in the same way, shift their attention to leaders who are producing results. A question for leaders with this mind-set is, are you producing the results or are you leading others to produce results?

Because You Help Others Achieve Results

People truly engage with leaders who help them to get better at what they do. This is the level where real leadership and followership kicks in. The focus here is on helping employees be the best they can so that they can succeed individually and collectively.

Because of Your Reputation

This is the ultimate level of followership, and very few achieve it. At this level people follow you because of who you are. Many of the followers are unknown to the leader who achieves this level. Notably, this type of leader is usually very humble and focused on the greater community—think of the likes of Nelson Mandela.

Why do your employees follow you? Better yet, what mindset are you operating with?

The idea of patriarchy can be very disconcerting, because we equate it with autocratic leadership and again hold this as a synonym for dictatorship. We need to shatter this errant logic system and realize that a bad leader or two does not make this true in all cases. The Middle East respects the role of centralized leadership found in the father, sheikh, or tribal chief. The region is a leader-centric environment—so lead!

TIP #7:

THANK GOD IT'S FRIDAY

Thank God it's Friday takes on a whole new meaning in the Middle East. It is much more than a substitution for the Western idea of Saturday, considering the modified workweek in most parts of the Middle East being Sunday to Thursday. Realizing that *family* is the significance of Friday in Middle Eastern culture is essential for leadership impact. Why does the family dynamic have such a powerful influence in the corporate setting in the region? Because the Arab world is a paternalistic society that is family focused.

Reading the decade-old guidebook *Don't They Know It's Friday?* or its equivalent is a mere beginning to understanding the significance of Friday in the region. Leaders need to move beyond the cultural insights and etiquette guidance that is found in these books and comprehend what the weekend represents in this society—specifically "family day," which is like a weekly version of Christmas, but on steroids.

The idea of "family day" accurately symbolizes how unique Middle Eastern culture really is, and it portrays the prominence of the group dynamic. Every week, the whole family (brothers, sisters, aunts, uncles, and cousins) gathers at the patriarch's house for an extended lunch and a day of lively discussions. This simple and precious act highlights the role of group interaction in every day life.

More than in the West, the influence of family in the Middle East is very strong and exerts tremendous influence over how people lead and what employees are looking for in their leaders. At the very least, organizations need to be aware of this influence. The business environment is a replica of this family structure: employees look to their boss for strong leadership and expect to experience what they would at home. At the same time, the boss embraces the responsibility for the stewardship of the employees.

An Arab family is a very tight-knit group of people, and the extended family is the locus for most social interaction, creating a strong group orientation. Family members have a say in an individual's major life decisions, such as education, work, and marriage. They live life out as a group, so much so that it is quite common to find cousins as best friends. In the Arab world, all of life, including business, is based on such relationships. So leading must be as well.

Although in the Middle East this social model is unfortunately slowly deteriorating, the reach of the extended family into other institutions and spheres of life will be a fixture for a good time to come. This is why it should never be ignored. When a close family member—even a senior leader's family member—circulates in the office, it is often regarded as distracting to an outsider who has not yet become wholly familiar with local culture.

The idea of group orientation and relationships does not merely stem from the influence of the family. Unity is an Islamic practice that is expressed in the concept of the *Ummah*. This identifies the community of all believers who are joined as they touch the ground together during prayer. The *Ummah* is universal and indivisible, representing in a real sense a "body." This idea clearly proposes a different positioning for individuals in relation to others as a collective group. Value comes from participation together in the *Ummah* rather than from individual practice.

Traditional Islamic values, as well as strong tribal and family orientations, influence the way business is conducted. The Middle East is a collectivist culture in which the group continues to protect the individuals, from their birth throughout their lifetime, in exchange for unquestionable loyalty. Consequently, employees in such societies highly value group interaction and seek strong attachment to their organizations and leaders. This strong cultural element carries over into the business environment. The employees' value and identity in large part come from the relationship network of which they are part.

THE "I" IN "WE"

On the surface, the group-individual dynamic can seem paradoxical to an outsider. While authority in the region ultimately rests on a single patriarch, that figure nonetheless is supposed to take the family opinion into account when making decisions. The result is an environment that can be surprisingly conducive to mutual consultation for major family decisions.

The family enjoys an active role in each family member's life in deciding whom to marry, where to work and live, and even what type of car to drive, among other matters. Because of this, some expatriates wrongly criticize their native counterparts for not making timely decisions. To do so is to misunderstand the real purpose behind people's behavior. Employees from this region act and interact within the decision-making processes of recognizable groups, looking to the patriarch for the final decision. He provides the purpose and modalities of each important decision.

I still laugh when I think about buying my first new car after marrying into an Arab family. As a young professional, I would decide what car I wanted, buy it, and then tell my dad I got a new car.

One day we were at my in-laws for lunch, which is not a simple small gathering, when my wife announced to her family that I was thinking of buying a new car. A firestorm of opinions as to what car, where to buy it, and so on started flying across the table. I leaned back from the table and silently laughed as my wife's brother, sister, cousins, nephews, parents, and even some people that I didn't even know were relatives passionately gave their opinion and took an active role in what car I should drive. Yet none of *them* were paying for it! In the end, I conformed and decided it would be wise to consider my father-in-law's counsel, as it appeared to be the "group" thing to do.

The impact of relationships is felt in practically every facet of life, including the way that business is carried out. It is, in a sense, *how* business is typically carried out—based predominantly upon relationships. In this highly relationship-oriented society, each family works toward the long-term accumulation of position, prestige, standing, relationship, and respect. As a result, in organizations, locals typically expect their leaders to adopt a patriarchal approach, while expatriates expect self-sufficiency and personal initiative to overcome challenges.

The business context is hierarchal and consultative at the same time. The result is that consultation can shape decision-making processes in significant ways. Muslims are encouraged to decide their affairs in consultation with those who will be affected by that decision. As a concept and longstanding local institution, *shura*—meaning "consultation"—is fundamentally different from other highly formalized political processes around the world. The irony is that it also breathes structure into the informal interactions within either family or business—certainly more so than in the West.

Two national cultural dimensions, collectivism and individualism, have been frequently used to understand how cultural dimensions impact human behavior. They have been frequently used in organizational psychology to understand cultures' impact upon human psychology and human behavior. The polarity of these cultural dimensions is primarily due to recognition that theories in management and organizational psychology have been based on individualistic cultures and may or may not be valid in other cultures.

In general, management theories are aligned with the Euro-American cultures that tend to be individualistic. The tendency of Euro-American cultures to be individualistic in orientation stems in part from an environment where self-reliance is highly valued. People from this orientation tend to be more self-centered and think of themselves as individuals and as distinct from others.

Given the "family" influence creating a group culture, leaders need to understand that "I" is never separated from "we" and as a result should leverage the group norm to positively impact performance and belonging.

STAY OR GO?

Typically, in Western society, parents raise their children so that they will go off to a university, and upon graduation become independent and live away from home. Deep down, mothers and fathers in the West strategize and work for their children to leave home when they turn eighteen. Just think of the scenes in American movies that show adult children (in their twenties) moving back in with Mom and Dad. How do those parents react? You can see the disgust and horror on the parents' faces as they are inconvenienced by this reality. Immediately they go back to working to help the child reclaim his or her independence.

As strange and harsh as it sounds, in Western society, parents pride themselves on raising their children to be independent and to live away from the home, away from the tribe. Thinking back on my own upbringing, which was in the mainstream, I'm not sure there was really any option other than packing up my stuff to go off to college and later to independently enter the world. Deep down, parents feel like they have failed when this doesn't happen, and they certainly brag when "little Johnny" is off on his own.

But in Arab society it is shameful and inconceivable to kick children out of their homes. Just as Western parents are saying good-bye, Arab parents nearly *require* that their children stay home until they are married, and then may even encourage their son or daughter to bring home a new spouse to live with them, or at least next door. Arab fathers take pride in the familial relations model.

The experience of one of my good friends is a good example. After finishing his law degree in Lebanon and spending a few years gaining practical experience, Nabil, headed off to complete his masters degree in law in the United Kingdom. Upon finishing, he returned to Beirut, moved back in with his parents, passed the bar exam, and set up his own law practice, which took off with immediate success.

After a few more years of working, around the age of twenty-nine, he decided it was time to move out on his own. When he broke the news to the family, Nabil's father responded, "Why so soon? Why do you want to move out now? Wait until you are married." Nabil gave some sort of explanation.

Then, with a quizzing look on his face, his dad asked, "What did your mom do to you? I can fix it."

"Nothing," replied Nabil.

Then the bribery set in; his dad offered to get him a new TV, change his bedroom, or do practically anything that Nabil might ask. At this point, in an attempt to convince his father that it was OK for him to move out, he took him over to the window and said, "Dad, see that building up the street? That is where I am moving to." Even though it was just a few buildings away, his parents were still devastated that he was moving out and claiming his independence.

These parenting approaches carry over into underlying management thought. The Western management style pushes employees to become independent; the focus is to reduce the dependence on the manager as quickly as possible. It is both a motivational strategy and a vote of confidence. Conversely, in the Arab world, the group identity and connection, the sense of belonging, is foundational. This carries into the workplace as well.

Can you imagine the shock and frustration when these two approaches collide, which they readily do? Let's look to Mike and Mohammed to see what happens in reality.

Mike, as an expatriate manager in Saudi Arabia, was very concerned about "Saudization"; he took it personally. So he told his Human Resources department that he wanted to hire a fresh Saudi graduate for a particular vacancy. Having his heart in the right place, Mike was committed, and looking forward, to grooming this recruit into a strong future leader for the company.

Mike was actively involved in the interview process, meeting each candidate himself. When he met Mohammed, he knew he was the one to hire. Mohammed had all of the tangible requirements—the right degree, high test scores, a good psychometric profile, and so on. In addition, he had the intangibles that Mike could not put his finger on, but his gut said "yes." Mike liked Mohammed a lot, and had a very good feeling about him.

Mohammed was even looking forward to working for and learning from Mike. He thought Mike was genuinely interested in him and in helping his career grow. Everyone could tell that Mike was taking this seriously, and not addressing nationalization as a tax, like many do.

As they started working together, Mike spent considerable time with Mohammed to help him get started, learn the ways of the company, and build his private-sector achievement since he was a first-generation corporate citizen. Everything seemed to be going well.

At least, that is, until the relationship began deteriorating, unaware to each of them at first.

One day Mohammed came to Mike and presented an idea for a project. Liking the idea—and even more, Mohammed's confidence—Mike said, "Go for it!" and sent him on his way. It was very similar to the way that a parent in the West bravely sends his or her child out into the world at eighteen years of age to stake independence.

The next day, Mohammed came into see Mike asking all sorts of questions. At first Mike answered a few, but then he pushed Mohammed away to go out and independently get the job done. As these episodes continued, each time Mike would tell Mohammed that he believed in him, that he could do it; then he would send him back out. Mike was practicing a leadership style that came very naturally to him, pushing his employees to be independent.

But what do you think Mohammed was feeling? Without meaning any harm, Mike was giving a subliminal message that he did not really care or have the time that Mohammed felt he needed.

Mohammed started wondering, "Why is my boss not giving me face anymore? He used to have ample time to teach and mentor me; he was like a dad at work."

And Mike started to second-guess his selection and his belief in Mohammed. He wondered why Mohammed was not able to perform independently.

While both men were well-intended the relationship broke down. Mike was pushing Mohammed to go on his own, but Mohammed was looking for support from his boss. This story is lived out day after day across the Middle East. A secret to success is to understand how parental and familial models shape the way we lead and want to be led.

An imported individualistic cultural model from a multinational corporation or Western orientation lacks validity in the group-oriented Arab market. Accordingly, leaders ought to consider what this variation in orientation means for leadership strategies and approaches. Employees coming from a group-orientation background expect and require much interaction with and "face" from their manager, and the amount they receive impacts their engagement in work.

In contrast, expatriate leaders often revert to a model that has proven successful at home. Unfortunately, many of them not only try to impose their imported ideals but expect locals to adopt them, which can pose a serious organizational problem. For example, a move toward individualism in the workplace on the part of many expatriate leaders is juxtaposed to the dynamics of honor and shame in the local business culture. Expatriate leaders need to temper colonialist leanings and to understand the local culture, be sensitive to and respect it, and learn how to be the best leaders possible within these parameters.

I LIKE YOU BECAUSE YOU ARE LIKE US

The practice of favoritism is understandable; the norm of hiring people who are most "like us" is a practical reality and very comfortable. The idea of cronyism, or the overlapping Arabic term *wasta*—showing partiality to long-standing friends by appointing them to positions of authority regardless of their qualifications—is not a new practice and is not unique to the Middle East.

The practice in the Middle East is a bit different from classic cronyism, but the elements remain true—giving partiality to likeness rather than deciding purely on capability. In this region it is obvious that managers give partiality to people who they think are like them. And I am not referring to nationalization. The hiring and promoting of people based upon "I like you because you are like us" is much more widespread outside of the nationalist camps.

Over coffee, a friend shared with me that since the arrival of its new CEO from South Africa, his organization had hired five senior managers also from his same country. I am sure that if we set up a blog, nearly every one of us would have a story to share.

OK, let's be honest. We do like being with people who are most like us. So, if this is such a common practice, why is it risky?

It may be true that it is easier as managers to work with people who are most like "us," because it is believed that they have quicker understanding of how we think, accept our behavior, and get the inside jokes. But this separation alienates the rest of the workforce. How much fun is it being an outsider?

Employees want to work in an environment where people with real ability can and do succeed. But there are views in the region that if you do not belong to a particular group (the favored one), your promotion opportunities are gravely limited. Since the workforce is very young, this favoritism (or perceived favoritism) plays against building loyalty in the workforce. Employees want to be treated fairly regardless of their background, with promotions that are based upon merit and performance.

Finally, it is quite demotivating to see someone hold a position for which he or she is inadequate. I hold to the view that employees want to be a part of a winning team and to work with high-caliber colleagues. When they question the ability of their peers and make derogatory judgments related to cronyism, it lowers the productivity of the whole team.

This becomes extremely challenging for you as a leader, where in the Middle East friends are not forgotten. So you are leading in an environment that has competing priorities taking place, on one hand the desire for recognition based upon merit, and on the other hand recognition of friendship—it is a relational society. As a leader, you need to bring these together in a way that one will not disrupt the other.

BUILDING THE TRIBE

Building the *tribe*, which is a regionalization of the word *team*, is one of the key leadership actions and needs to be a priority for every CEO, managing director, and business leader in the Middle East. This region is historically and in many senses still a tribal society, meaning that it is largely organized on the basis of kinship.

Central to building a senior management team—or, for that matter, any team—is participation. Of course the leader needs to actively participate, but not just in the leader–team member interaction as reflected in the prevalent spoke-and-hub model. The leader needs to emphasize member-integrated participation.

Interviews with numerous senior managers reveal the spoke-and-hub model as one of the primary team dysfunctions in the Middle East. In a wheel, the spokes only interact with one another through the hub (figuratively, the leader) or the rim (meetings or assigned projects). While this may make a wheel function properly, it is far from ideal for a team, because when the majority of the interaction is between the leader and team members versus among the team members, it causes the team to come out of balance, just as asymmetries of mass cause a tire to wobble.

I'm emphasizing this point because many leaders see what appears as participation when looking at it from where they sit. Through the participants or an outsider's eyes, however, it becomes clear that the consistent participation is with the leader, but that it is not regular among team members.

Team members confess that they willingly come together when the need requires, but immediately thereafter they return back to their own "silo"—the department or division. So instead of working as a team, they are only creating working groups. The repercussion is that the business becomes a conglomeration of senior members who operate with their department's "silo" first. The leader must take accountability and take action to encourage cross-integration. As in a tribe, a business leader needs to build collective participation that is direct between team members.

Role clarity and expectations are another characteristic of tribes. While member-integrated participation is critical, this does not mean that being a team requires everyone to plan everything together, to discuss everything, and to decide everything collectively. A team differs from a "peewee" football match in which every kid runs after the ball, forgetting about his or her position and related contribution to the team's success.

In a tribe each member has a role and responsibility upon which other members are dependent. In a tribe you find hunters, gatherers, a chief, a shaman, and tribal elders. When building the tribe, the leader needs to take an active role in helping other leaders and employees understand the dichotomy between performing clear team roles and emphasizing member-integrated participation.

For leaders, the key is *building* the tribe, not just being a good tribe/team member. This requires connecting employees to one another and the organization, achieving consensus and cohesion, and promoting collaborative work to achieve mutually beneficial goals. Unfortunately, many organizational practices grind against the grain of connectivity to promote silos—and worse, individualism. Consider how key performance indicators are used in your company. Most likely they are focused on individual achievement and reviewed in a spoke-and-hub model in which the leader and employee review is independent of that of the other team members. This is far from the way that a tribe functions. In a tribe there is mutual accountability; the individuals help each other achieve and more so hold each other accountable to deliver what is needed. Honor and shame, by nature, are collective concepts.

The social context and connection is very real in the Middle East, much more so than in other parts of the world. A question for determining if you are leading as "I" or "we" is, do your leaders and employees measure their success through collective or through personal achievement?

The Arab world revolves around the family as a group; the collective identity is greater than that of the individual member. Building a tribe from your workforce is an unrealized opportunity that leaders need to leverage. Employees saying they "belong" to your company fail inconsideration to having a true group identity. Leadership success demands that you become a leader of a cohesive group rather than a mere collection of individuals.

TIP #8:

REALIZE THAT DIVERSITY IS MULTIDIMENSIONAL

This tip is unique to the Gulf Cooperation Council (GCC), which enjoys one of the most diverse workforces in the world. Employees come from over two hundred countries and it is common to find twenty—even thirty or more—nationalities represented in a single organization, each employee bringing with him or her vastly different backgrounds and experiences. In a few organizations, the number reaches up to a 150 different nationalities. The workforce in the GCC employs more nationalities than the United Nations has member nations.

Hussein A. Al-Banawi, chairman of Banawi Industrial Group (BIG) in Saudi Arabia, emphasizes diversity by saying, "At BIG, when the national anthem is played, we have to play twenty-five different versions to represent all of our workforce."

In practicality, the GCC workforce is the dictionary definition of diversity. When it comes to leading in the Middle East, diversity means more than nationality. It also represents all aspects of the workforce's background, including education levels, age, experience, and corporate exposure.

Many leaders find it tricky to make sense of so much diversity, as there are numerous imported nationalities in the society. With the numerous nationalities come different sights, smells, attitudes, driving patterns, religions, parenting approaches, thoughts on business, educational backgrounds, and so forth, but all are clothed in similarities. Whether one comes from London, Sydney, Shanghai, New York, Delhi, Nairobi, or any of the other major cities, many of the same consumer brands (for example, HSBC, McDonald's, BP, and Starbucks) are observable, and there are striking surface similarities. The appearance may seem confusing because what is observed and what is lived may appear contradictory.

Diversity is the great advantage for a business in the GCC it reemerges as the global hub for trade, a tourism hot spot, and an ambitious home for sports and culture. But you need to understand it.

Successful leadership in the GCC means more than simply knowing Arab culture and understanding how to address someone respectfully. Business leaders need to understand how to communicate from one culture to another to be able to respond to the specific needs of each team member. It is important to note that leaders need not only be aware of the differences across the diverse workforce but also how to communicate with understanding to each. Leaders who are successful at this understand and sense different individual perspectives, cultures, and expectations so that there is a level of respect, trust, and understanding—from everyone's perspective—underpinning the working relationships that are established with colleagues, peers, and clients.

GEOGRAPHY OF DIVERSITY

An employee's first language will give you a sneak peek into how he or she thinks about and understands things. I am not proposing that leaders run off and learn thirty different languages, but they should not overlook the value of understanding the nature and structure of their employees' native languages. Since language reveals how people think, if one understands a language, by default he or she will learn the thinking style and as a result be able to communicate better. The key point for leaders is to understand that an employee's first language highlights how that person thinks differently from you do. Recent research has confirmed that there is geography of thought and that people from different parts of the world think differently. When a leader understands how an employee thinks, that leader will be able to communicate better and as a result motivate the employee to perform at his or her best.

The socioeconomic environment in which expatriates and locals were brought up affects the way they approach and view business relationships, priorities, and ultimate objectives. The background of the employee influences motivation, reward systems, performance, interpersonal relations, evaluation schemes, time frames, and the like. Leaders who underestimate these differences run the risk of losing valuable talent; this is especially dangerous in times of scarce talent and fierce competition. But as one reflects on the differentiators, it is important not to fall into the dangerous pitfall of thinking that one particular approach is superior to another. Both perspectives have great value; success will only come as leaders leverage both views for the insights into the workforce.

BE AN EXPATRIATE EXPERT

Do you want to be a great leader in the GCC? Then you need to learn how to lead expatriates; there is no escaping it. It makes no difference if you are an expatriate or national; leadership success in the region is largely dependent on the ability to lead expatriates.

Whether right or wrong, the workplace in the GCC is chockfull of expatriates. The percentage of expatriates in the private sector is probably the highest around the world. By expatriates, I am not referring only to the common expatriate stereotype, meaning Western professionals, but to anyone who has left his or her native country and come to the Middle East for work.

In the broadest sense, an expatriate is a person who is temporarily or permanently residing in a country or culture other than that of his or her upbringing or legal citizenship. In common practice, the term is often used in the context of professionals sent abroad by their companies, as opposed to locally hired staff. But I like to think of expatriates as people who are "not from here."

Every leader needs to become an expert in leading expatriates, as this is the day-to-day reality of leading in the region. Not only does your success as a leader depend on your ability to lead expatriates, so does your organization's success. According to research, the failure rate of expatriates, the ones who leave their company in the first year, averages 30 percent. Failure does not just mean turnover; it also means a loss of expected productivity, as in the first year of an expatriate assignment the costs are high and the productivity is very low. This is true from the CEO to the janitor. Additionally, 24 percent of all expatriate assignments end prematurely.

Adjustments to the culture represent a significant concern when employing expatriates. These adjustments are general in regard to adapting to the new host country and specific relating to the work environment. In the GCC it is even more complex, as expatriates have to adjust to their coworkers' cultures as well. At first, they commonly feel like outsiders. There is one thing consistent about expatriates: no matter where they are from, where they are working, and what they do, they are not home. Leaders have an opportunity to create an environment of belonging. The depth of belonging an employee feels at work has a connection to how well he or she performs on the job.

Perhaps the greatest cost consideration for an organization is expatriates who are not effective yet remain in their positions. Expatriate effectiveness needs to be of top priority to every leader.

How a leader leads has a direct impact on employee performance. So to maximize your leadership in the GCC, you need to be an expatriate expert.

MULTILINGUAL IN ONE LANGUAGE

It is easy to be tricked by the fact that everyone is speaking the same language and to equate this with common understanding. In the GCC, most people speak English in the work environment, but not everyone's English has the same or common meaning, because for most it is a second or even third language.

Just because everyone is speaking the same language, leaders should not assume that the common language means common understanding; leaders need to become "multilingual in one language." The meaning that is attached to words varies greatly between cultures. To master being multilingual in one language—meaning, when speaking a common language ensure common understanding from the listeners' background—leaders need to shift their attention from what they are saying to what will be understood.

Assuming common understanding because we are speaking a common language can, and often does, result in real confusion.

When I first moved to Dubai, I wanted a swimming pool and wasn't overly concerned about the house—well, actually I was, but still the swimming pool was the priority. I set out on an arduous pool-with-a-house hunt by turning to the classified section of the newspaper.

This is the beginning point of the confusion, even though I was reading in English what was written in English. As I looked in the paper I saw choices for "flats" or "villas." But I wanted a "house." Having lived in Beirut for years, I had already come to learn that "flat" meant apartment. And when I drove around Dubai I saw houses. So, I concluded by process of elimination that a villa must be a house. Although where I come from a villa is a country home or a summer vacation rental.

When I contacted the real estate agent and told her, a native English speaker, that I wanted a villa with a pool, she responded "And a garden?" I stopped her midsentence and said, "I do not want a garden." My emphatic no put her into a state of confusion. I thought, "Why is she asking me about a garden?" Of course I didn't want to have a garden in Dubai!

As our banter continued she asked me again, "You want a villa with a pool, but don't want a garden?" She seemed very uncertain as she asked me this. In an attempt to be very clear, I repeated, "I want a villa with a pool and perhaps a small yard."

REALIZE THAT DIVERSITY IS MULTIDIMENSIONAL

Then we realized that therein lay the confusion.

For me, a garden was the patch in the back of the yard where each summer my parents tore up the perfectly good grass, planted seeds in the ground, and spent the rest of the summer watering the garden and pulling out weeds so that in August they could pick a few tomatoes and other vegetables. I was not about to undertake all of that in the intensity of desert heat. All I wanted was a swimming pool with grassy area where the kids could play—a yard. The real estate agent's meaning of the common word *garden* was very different from my understanding.

Two native English speakers were confusing and frustrating each other while thinking they were speaking perfectly clearly. How much more so do you think the confusion can be when speaking in a second language?

This simple example illustrates why it is imperative that leaders are multilingual in one language. Can you imagine the depth of confusion that transpires on the job when communicating to a workforce coming from a multitude of countries? Have you ever given a project to an employee only to have him or her come up with something that is entirely different from your expected results? Perhaps it comes down to understanding. Great leaders understand the need to communicate clearly, especially with the diverse and multidimensional workforce in the GCC.

When it comes to workplace communication, leaders often use terse, straight-to-the-point language; the connectivity of meaning is stripped out, especially when it comes to the performance language of KPIs (key performance indicators) and SMART (specific, measurable, achievable, relevant, and time-bound) goals. Most front-line employees (individual contributors) in the GCC come from the emerging markets (and make up the majority of the workforce). They are from oral cultures, and are accustomed to finding direction and meaning through the stories that are told. Asian emerging market employees (people from the Middle East, GCC, Central Asia, the subcontinent, and further east) rely on how verbs are used and how objects relate to one another to communicate and understand meaning. This is juxtaposed to Westerners, who categorize objects and rely on nouns as the basis of language.

As you will see in Tip #10, "Have a Cup of Coffee," communication in the region is often informal and full of stories. Given that we are in an oral culture, a simple piece of advice for leading in business is to become really good at telling a story. The value of being multilingual in one language is recognizing the difference between communicating in an oral versus a literary tradition.

The core concept of communication is making sure that the audience receives the intended message. This is exactly what being multilingual in one language is all about: realizing that your audience could have ten to fifteen different native languages all communicating in a second tongue. Therefore, you need to be doubly sure that you are communicating clearly.

Diversity, real diversity, as experienced in the GCC is creating perhaps the greatest management challenge in modern business history. Diversity is usually made up of a few, at most, perspectives—black and white or male and female, for example. In the Middle East, the aspects of diversity are too numerous to count and diversity goes greatly beyond what traditional programs address. Great leaders in the GCC become multilingual in one language.

TIP #9:

BE CAREFUL—THERE IS NO "GET OUT OF JAIL FREE" CARD

Although the Middle East has been dominated by the real estate sector, as in the game Monopoly, there is one big difference—here there is no "Get Out of Jail Free" card. The rapid growth in the region has brought in the unwanted (but commonly accompanied) issue of corruption. The newspapers and court records provide a multitude of instances where business leaders became careless and landed on the "Go to Jail" space or drew the "Go Directly to Jail, Do Not Pass Go, Do Not Collect $200" card. Successful leadership in the Middle East requires spotless integrity.

Throughout history, fast-growth environments have been bastions for corporate corruption and, unfortunately, today's Middle East is no exception. In rapidly growing first-generation corporate societies, temptations do present themselves—the jails are full of corporate leaders who tried to take advantage of the opportunities yet failed.

Unfortunately, there has always been and will continue to be a risk-growth trade-off. Corruption is a risk associated with fast growth. Because one of the things this region needs—this *world* needs—is more growth, the reality of corruption will continue to exist. It will continue so much so that a leading business school believes that Harvard is a business school of the past since students need to be ready for the unpredictable, sometimes corrupt, world of the emerging economies. The business school of the future has to be different from those in existence today. It has to be prepared to work with the risk of corruption.

The primary driver for corruption in fast-growth markets is an environment that fosters greediness and the desire to get things done at any cost. Are most leaders greedy, and do they think that the ends should justify the means? This is not a flattering prospect, and most readers would desire that it not be so and that such a situation could be avoided. The fact is that while not all leaders are corrupt, the ones involved in (or thinking about) corrupt practices in one way or the other, either due to greed or so-called compulsion, are tarnishing the image of many.

If a leader is unlucky enough to land on the "Go to Jail" space, it will take more than rolling doubles to get out. Most of the legal systems in first-generation corporate societies do not operate on the premise of "innocent until proven guilty." And as a leader, the risk of ending up in jail without a "Get Out of Jail Free" card is a far greater one, disproportionate to the potential rewards from engaging in corruption.

HONOR AND SHAME

Leaders need to actively avoid corruption, or even the appearance of such—they need spotless integrity. In this region, disputes are settled, interests are pursued, and justice and order are

BE CAREFUL—THERE IS NO "GET OUT OF JAIL FREE" CARD

maintained according to "honor and shame." The key isn't just to *act* rightly or wrongly; honor signifies respect and doing things according to group values.

From this example we learn a key to leading in the region: lead with the value of honor and shame, not from the perspective of guilt and innocence. Sociologists have recognized that three social values have existed since the earliest of times: fear, shame, and guilt. They are the building blocks of society, and each has a different importance depending on the cultural makeup of that society.

The West predominantly operates with the value of "guilt and innocence," which is the basis for most modern management practices. In other words, something is either right or wrong. Just consider the fact that most Western films are built upon the framework of the "good guys" versus "the bad guys."

Guilt and innocence are such an integral part of Western society and its practice of religion that Westerners often cannot imagine a world where right versus wrong isn't the accepted basic underlying principle. It is the yardstick by which everything else is measured. They talk about the rightness and wrongness of a person's actions; they are obsessed with knowing their rights and exercising them. Almost every major issue the West struggles with involves an aspect of deciding whether something is right or wrong. The pulls and demands of these two diametrically opposed forces dictate much of Western human behavior.

However, not everyone in the world operates within this paradigm. As I mentioned earlier, Arabs and Arab society operate from another dimension—that of honor and shame. While there is an awareness of guilt, it does not have the same power and influence as shame does. The Westerner tries to act correctly, while the Arab would try to act honorably, not shamefully.

The underlying principle in the Middle East is that there are honorable and dishonorable ways of doing things. The secret isn't whether you act rightly or wrongly; in the Arab world, there are hundreds of nuances that communicate messages about shame and honor. Everywhere you move, there is honor—who sits in what chair, who goes through the door first, who is on the right-hand side. It is not about the "correct" way to do things but about the honorable way to act.

In an Arab society, wherever you go, you represent your family and tribe (or loyalties). So you are not free to act as you may, because if you act shamefully, then the family or tribe is affected. You can think of guilt as being more about your personal feelings and you as an individual, whereas shame is about the impact on a group. In an honor-and-shame culture, you must always act honorably so that the honor of your family or group is upheld. For honor to work it must be attached to something greater than the individual.

If someone is from a tribe, he thinks and acts and dresses as a tribesman. His actions reflect the honor of the tribe. And if he acts shamefully, the whole tribe is shamed.

Shame is the aversion to disgrace and the defense of honor. Honor is to guide a leader's conduct in friendships, in private life, and in the work and public environments. On the other hand, honor is also the esteem in which a leader is held by the group he or she leads—it is the recognition by the leader's group that the leader is a valuable member of that group. In this regard, honor means having the respect of others.

The respect-oriented society stems from the overarching worldview of honor and shame rather than the guilt and innocence of the West. Locals are proud of their Arabic and Islamic traditions, and they anchor their business culture in these elements.

While honor signifies respect for being the kind of person and doing the kinds of things the group values, shame signifies being seen as less than valuable because one has behaved in a way that is contrary to the values of the group. If a leader loses the respect of society, his or her worth is lost; in other words, the leader "loses face" and is viewed as a disgrace. On the other hand, shame can signify a positive character trait—sensitivity to the opinion of the group so much so that the leader avoids actions that could bring disgrace. For example, a leader might avoid partaking in a personal yearning because of the awareness of what such action would bring to the group's reputation.

The concept of honor and shame can be traced back to the early Bedouin code of practice, which existed even before Islam arrived. This code is still very much in existence today, and it affects not only the way individuals act but the actions of entire nations. An example was when King Abdullah bin Abdulaziz Al Saud of Saudi Arabia chastened US president Barack Obama on honor during the Arab street uprisings. Is your leadership characterized by right and wrong or by honor and shame?

LOYALTY

Although it is not against the law and will not land you in a physical jail, a lack of loyalty will find you estranged from the tribe. Tip #7, "Thank God It's Friday," emphasized that in an Arab family there is an expectation of unquestionable loyalty. Out of this relational and honor-based society comes an intense focus on loyalty. It is expected and often guaranteed because leaders surround themselves with subordinates they can trust.

Loyalty is a two-way street: the chief expects loyalty from the tribe, the leader from his or her followers, and in turn they reciprocate with loyalty—unless the tribe member breaks the code of loyalty by acting shamefully, which may result in being shunned. In the Arab world, friends are not forgotten.

The influence of the family is central to understanding the Arab manager's use of time during the workday. When a close family member appears at the office of even a very senior manager, it is regarded as improper for the demands of organizational hierarchy to take precedence over family obligations. In other words, that senior manager will prioritize giving honor to his or her family over work. Loyalty is the first and greatest lesson taught in an Arab household.

Loyalty is willing in that it is freely given, not coerced. But it is not a foregone conclusion or granted without merit. Given the first-generation corporate society, don't expect instant and unearned loyalty to the organization, or even to you as the leader. Loyalty is developed and built with trust. When leading in the Middle East, remember the unfortunate truth that trust and loyalty are lost much faster than they are built. And when they are lost, they are lost forever!

DIGNITY

Over lunch one day, Sheikh Mohammed Abdullah bin Mubarak Al Sabah, the minister of state for cabinet affairs in Kuwait, shared with me his view of the problematic Arab Spring. He was quick to point out that the issue was not driven by political interference, autocratic rule, or even unemployment, as most commentators conclude. His strong hypothesis is that the uprisings were caused by dignity—actually, a lack of dignity. The underlying cause, from Mohammed Bouazizi of Tunisia setting himself on fire, to the protests in Cairo's Tahrir Square, Bahrain, and even Syria, was a crying out to be recognized—a crying out for dignity.

BE CAREFUL—THERE IS NO "GET OUT OF JAIL FREE" CARD

Echoing this insight, a Syrian caller to an Al Jazeera program said, "We don't want a thousand five hundred lira; we want a thousand five hundred units of dignity." Dignity is the innate right to be treated respectfully. When dignity is spoken of, it is often used to suggest that someone is not receiving a proper degree of respect.

Discussing with Sheikh Mohammed his premise that the cause of the uprising in the streets was a plea for dignity led me to think about what dignity means in the workplace. If dignity is such a fiery issue among the jobless, is it a hot issue for the gainfully employed? Yes, it is. Employees also want to be recognized and treated with respect.

While governments and the private sector are working to create jobs, the issue of dignity needs to be a top-priority action item, as these young people have the potential to release years of pent-up frustration into the workplace. There should be wide recognition that if nothing is done, dignity levels could dissipate in the workforce and bring another Arab Spring uprising—but this time among your workforce.

So what can you do to build dignity?

Leaders need to build respectful relationships with their employees—all of them—and among the different groups within the workforce. As hard as this is in a hierarchical environment, the need exists to break down the idea of "us" and "them" or "suits" and "troops." Treating people with respect on a daily basis is one of the most helpful actions a leader can take to offset tension in the workplace. Respect is an action—leaders must show respect by acting and speaking respectfully.

How can leaders bring the topic of respect to the forefront? By taking an interest in others. This is more than making statements like "Everyone is important, from the tea boy to our senior leaders." Taking an interest means taking the time to listen to what others have to say and recognizing that their insights count. Additionally, you build respect by allowing your employees to choose their own actions.

Dignity is a state in which all employees have the opportunity to succeed but that can only be actualized through hard work and performance. The unfortunate "elephant in the room" that is cronyism, wasta, and the hierarchy of passports stands in the way of equal opportunities. These practices need to be set aside.

Finally, you build dignity by understanding that the face of dignity has a regional look. Culture, family, and peer social relationships influence the perception of dignity, and in the Middle East dignity is about honor and shame. The secret isn't to act rightly instead of wrongly; honor signifies respect for being the kind of person who does things according to group values.

Showing dignity is a critical responsibility for all leaders. While this seems obvious, it may not be as intuitive as you think. The challenge of building dignity in the workplace is big and urgent. Action is required now if we are to escape potentially dire circumstances.

HARAM

The question still looms: When something shameful—or even worse, downright wrong—happens, how do you respond? Do you immediately roll up your sleeves and take action, or do you adopt a wait-and-see approach?

Facing a crisis in business is never easy, and it is even harder in an honor-and-shame culture. However, the right thing to do is to roll up your sleeves and take action. This may mean going public about it when you might normally wait.

BE CAREFUL—THERE IS NO "GET OUT OF JAIL FREE" CARD

In times of crisis, it is very important for the leader to be physically present. It is not the time to hide away in a "war room." A leader's presence brings comfort and confidence to all of the concerned stakeholders. Being present allows leaders to receive the intelligence surrounding the crisis without it being filtered through the troops or the media.

Autocratic leaders do well in times of crisis, as quick decisions are usually needed. This is not the time for lengthy deliberations; rather, leaders need to make swift decisions.

A time of crisis is a time for action; it is not the time to patiently wait to see what will transpire and silently hope that the matter at hand will drift away. Action restores confidence, demonstrates to the public that there is leadership, and gives the impression that there will be a secure future.

Perhaps most important is the power of saying "I'm sorry." Leaders need to publicly, humbly, and boldly declare regret for the actions in these unfortunate times.

OATH OF LEADERSHIP

Leaders should make an oath of leadership freely and upon their honor, as being a leader is honorable and requires hard work, skill, rightful behavior, accountability, and responsibility. By taking this oath, leaders are declaring to their team, company, family, and the world that they will act as responsible and accountable leaders. And by practicing the contents of the oath, they will be respected and make a positive contribution to their employees, the shareholders, and society as a whole.

It is clearly time for an approach that includes reforming management and creating leaders who are responsible for their actions and the impact those actions might have on their organizations. In light of questionable corporate practices, it is time for leaders to pledge their responsibility for the life of their organizations and to greater society. Borrowing from the ancient practice of the Hippocratic oath all leaders should take an oath of leadership:

- I will be competent in my skills and actions while continually striving to improve my leadership.
- I will maintain and strengthen the vision of my organization and strive to be honorable in a way that is respectful and contributes to social growth.
- I will respect the rights and dignity of all people; I will hold accountable those employees to whom I have been entrusted with leadership responsibility, and I will provide opportunities for their growth.
- I will conduct myself with the highest level of integrity and take responsibility for my actions while laboring for the good of my organization and keeping myself and my leadership far from all intentional ill-doing, especially from damaging the economy, society, and environment. And I will oppose all forms of corruption and exploitation.

We are leading in a society that has a value system that goes beyond mere right and wrong." Don't focus on the correct way to act; instead, live honorably, and you can then sell your "Get Out of Jail Free" card. Honorable leading that brings dignity to others creates an environment in which you have nothing to worry about. Take an oath of leadership and proclaim it.

TIP #10:

HAVE A CUP OF COFFEE

Shortly after arriving in the Middle East, Scott, an expatriate, learned that the value of a cup of coffee is more than the needed caffeine.

Upon joining a company as a department head, he quickly realized that his and the department's success was going to be dependent on Nasser, a colleague who was leading a complementary (maybe we should even say overlapping) department. Simply stated, Nasser would either have a direct impact on Scott's success or stand in the way of his progress.

Realizing that Nasser had coffee every morning upon arriving in the office at 7:40 a.m., Scott decided to join him in his office. This could be seen as a waste of time in many settings, as they really did not discuss much. But Scott continued, and day after day he went to Nasser's office each morning to have coffee with his colleague. Not realizing what was really taking place at the time, Scott later realized he had been showing respect and building a relationship of trust.

Then one day, at 7:35 a.m., Nasser showed up in Scott's office and from that day onward took his coffee in Scott's office. After a few more days, Nasser started inviting his friends from work to Scott's office for coffee. This practice led to great and mutual success in the business.

What happened? Trust and respect were built because Scott invested time. Unfortunately, we hear of so many stories with different endings—all because time is not invested.

As a leader in the Middle East, you would be wise to remove your watch for a moment and adopt the practice of having a regular cup of coffee with your boss, employees, customers, and even prospective clients. The dividends from this practice far outweigh the anticipated loss of time. But don't limit the idea of having coffee only to coffee, as the practice can include tea, *shisha*, or a meal as well.

Since the fifteenth century and the earliest evidence of coffee drinking, the practice has been an integral part of Arab society. More important than the coffee itself is the prevalence of the coffee house and the daily ritual. Coffee is a way of life. Friends gather for hours over coffee to discuss the matters of the day, society, and the world. The routine is more of a cultural relic.

A visit to Falamanki, a café in the heart of Beirut, or any equivalent across the Arab world, will find every chair filled with people sitting for hours over coffee, snacks, and *shisha* while discussing the matters of life. On my first visit to a café in the region, I was shocked to see people talking, laughing, and carrying on the whole evening and into the night. It is clear that this lifestyle becomes a primary source of knowledge sharing, with people hotly debating the news, or the way things should be, and seeking opinions on matters of work.

HAVE A CUP OF COFFEE

Showing respect over coffee is an important part of Middle Eastern family culture, as exemplified in the practice of having a regular (usually daily) cup of coffee with one's father. In the West, it might seem the "right thing" to do to meet dad for coffee periodically. In Arab culture, it is the honorable thing to do to pass by dad's house daily for coffee; it happens without forethought, as if to imply, why would you think of doing otherwise?

When line managers recognize and practice the daily cup of coffee ritual in the workplace, they model a patriarchal style of management, and this practice results in effective workplace relationships, improved performance, and increased employee engagement and retention.

While I was having coffee with a senior leader from one of the region's leading companies, he shared with me how he had gone from being somewhat of a wall ornament to working on strategic projects.

John had worked for his company for around ten months as a director, but his relationship with the firm went back years, as he had previously been a consultant. Given what he perceived to be a good history with the company, he was shocked when, after joining full-time, he was set aside and not encouraged to contribute; his expertise wasn't even sought.

He remarked to me, "This changed when I accompanied one of our board members on a regional tour." Elaborating on the trip, John said, "It felt like all we did was have lunch and dinner each day. Never did we have more than one meeting in a day. We just spent time together over meals and coffee."

But when they returned to the home office, John noticed everything changed—he was no longer a wall ornament and was now an active team member contributing to several strategic initiatives.

10 TIPS FOR LEADING IN THE MIDDLE EAST

I asked, "Why the change?" and John replied, "Lunch and dinner." He realized that over the lunches and dinners, trust was built. What seemed to be an unproductive trip with limited activity proved to be a breakthrough for his future involvement.

How often do you skip an opportunity for coffee, lunch, or dinner because you are too busy or not interested?

Here in the Middle East, having coffee is about much more than the coffee. Where I come from, having a coffee is often about enjoying the coffee's taste (and getting the much-needed caffeine) and spending time casually with friends, but in the Middle East having coffee shows respect and value, and—most important—it is where trust is built.

Trust is the backbone of Arab society, and it is the currency of business. Trust is not built over random encounters or official business in the office; it is built, matured, and sustained over time. In Middle Eastern culture, one mechanism for this is spending time over a cup of coffee or tea. As difficult as this is to express in words, there is a relationship between time and trust. So returning to the heart of this tip, it is advised that you remove your watch or press *pause* on your stopwatch and invest time over coffee or a meal to build trust.

Actually, having a cup of coffee is the key to virtually all relationships in the Arab world.

Although this tip is focused primarily on leading in a regional business, multinational companies operating in the region would be wise to understand the rhythm of the market and the long-term impact that is lost in impetuous acts that try to force pressurized operating models.

A senior business development director for a multinational corporation told me of his meeting a key member of a royal

HAVE A CUP OF COFFEE

family and the ensuing lack of understanding from his firm's headquarters in the United States.

During this lunch, the sheikh expressed interest in the services of this company and gave the business development director his personal contact details. In his excitement, the director shared this news with his CEO, who responded with, "When will you close the deal—by the end of the quarter?"

Understanding the impact of time, the business development director responded, "After thirty cups of coffee." And the CEO pressured, "How long will that take?" To succeed in the Middle East, it is imperative to understand the impact of time and not limit yourself to days on a calendar.

The benefits of having a cup of coffee are the dividends of the time invested. Go order your latte or Arabic coffee today!

CONCLUSION

It is very clear that the myth, "there is one approach to leading and it is the same everywhere," is merely a myth. Our conversation highlighted the truth – that when the context changes so must the approach to leading. This is the silver thread through *10 Tips for Leading in the Middle East* connecting each tip together. And it is the initial piece of advice to heed.

From the first tip – Avoid Leadership Colonialism on through to making sure you have the right vehicle for the environment, even to have a cup of coffee, the need to adapt your leadership approach leaps from the pages. The challenge that you will face is going to work tomorrow and not settling back in to a leadership style that is so familiar. Why is this so true?

Largely because we are limited by our past experience, either from comfort or the belief that it brought success. This limitation reminds me of the Cheeseburger Theory.

If you have never eaten a cheeseburger and you go to McDonald's, will it be the best cheeseburger you have ever had? I know, I know – if you are a cheeseburger lover, like I am, you probably disagree that McDonalds is the best. But, if it is the only one that you have ever eaten, it has to be the best from you experience.

Then, why does the person who has never had a cheeseburger think McDonalds is the best, yet for you it is not the best? It is because you have broader experience and the cheeseburger rookie has no other point of reference, so in his or her mind it must be the best. It is easy to confuse a single experience with being the best experience even when in reality we know this is not true.

The principle is that people limit themselves by their own experience and exposure. Like the "cheeseburger theory," you may think your approach to leading is the only and best way. But, don't let your leading in the Middle East be limited by your past experience and concept of what the best is.

So, why do people eat cheeseburgers other than McDonalds? Someone had the courage to challenge the way things were done and convince others to try another cheeseburger at someplace better, say Shake Shack, and then through broader experience they realize that there is a better burger than their reference point.

(an excerpt from my book The Cheeseburger Theory and other leadership observations*)*

    Since you have the privilege of leading in the Middle East, I want to encourage you to enjoy it, make the most of it. Take the time to master leading first-generation corporate citizens and the youth bulge. For sure, you need to receive the soul while perceiving the appearance – one of the top mistakes that expats make is to live in their enclave and draw conclusions about the region through the eyes and experiences of other expats. Get to know the people – your employees, live out thank God it is Friday. One of the harder challenges when coming into the region is shifting from a focus on the value of the shares to what brings value to the shareholder – the legacy. This tip is tied to a bedrock principle in the region the role of the patriarch. Leadership success begins

CONCLUSION

with an understanding of the impact of the family structure and fatherly role. Set your perspectives aside for a moment and explore the region through another's eyes.

Now that we have finished our coffee conversation, practice the *10 Tips for Leading in the Middle East* and go have a cup of coffee!

Printed in Great Britain
by Amazon.co.uk, Ltd.,
Marston Gate.